I know first-hand that what Andre Butler has so powerfully laid out in God's Future For You works. What a blessing of the Lord to have these truths placed in a simple day-to-day format that anyone with a Bible and a heart's desire to prosper and be in health can follow. Have faith in God! Start today. Jesus is our future, and our future is bright. Jesus is Lord!

—*Kenneth Copeland, director, Kenneth Copeland Ministries*

I have known Andre Butler since he was a young boy and have watched him grow up into a fine minister of the Gospel. I got to know him personally a little more while he attended Rhema Bible Training Center and participated as a player for the Rhema Eagles, our collegiate basketball team. You will be encouraged about the good things that God has for you as you read God's Future for You. I know that it will be a help to all who read it.

—*Kenneth W. Hagin, president, Kenneth Hagin Ministries and Rhema Bible Training Center*

Pastor Andre Butler's book, God's Future for You, is a powerful resource that is designed to set you on the path to your destiny. Many times we end up on detours that take us away from God's will and delay our progress. However God's Future for You contains valuable insights that will help reveal God's vision for your life and propel you toward the future He has prepared for you. In this transforming book, you will receive the keys you need to fulfill God's unique purpose and will for your life.

—*Creflo Dollar, author, Winning in Troubled Times*

Andre Butler encourages you to embrace the special plans that God has for you and follow His path to a life of peace and fulfillment. God's Future for You shows how the decisions you make, the company you keep, the joy you express, and the impact you make on the world are all part of His dream for you. Jesus came to give you a choice and by following His way you can experience the amazing future He has specially designed for you.

—*Pastor Matthew Barnett, co-fr___ ___ ___ ___ Dream Center, and author of The ___ ___ 'thin You*

T0167344

God's Future For You is a must-read for the next generation to give them hope for their future. Our youth today need to understand that God has a brilliant master plan for their life in spite of the turmoil they see around the world. Andre Butler has allowed God to use him to inspire all who read this book to choose and experience abundant life for the rest of their lives!

—CeCeWinans, Recording Artist

I love the ministry of Pastor Andre Butler because he has a heart for people and he's relevant. My ministry is also about empowering and inspiring people. Pastor Andre's book, God's Future for You, does just that! Take it from me, once you realize how bright your future is, you'll never look back. I encourage you to take this challenge to see how amazing your life can be!

—Vickie Winans, recording Artist, songwriter, producer, and CEO of Viviane, Inc.

One who ponders these pages will be refreshed and changed. This is a delightfully readable and altogether profitable discussion of success in the believer's life: how to get there and continue to learn and grow. It's ideal for personal or group interaction.

—Lynne Hammond, pastor and author of The Master Is Calling

Many views concerning life are passed around today to ease the pain that humanity is suffering. Seldom do we stop long enough to understand and comprehend God's view. Pastor Andre Butler has proven himself as a disciple of the Lord with determination and character to push beyond the religious ideas that captivate the church world at large and actually comprehend the bigness of God's heart to experience a relationship with Him. You will be refreshed and gain insight into the relationship that God has planned for you. Get ready to experience fulfillment!

—Jim Hockaday, minister and author of Until I Come

God's **future** for you

God's **future** for you

see how
amazing
your life
can be

ANDRÉ BUTLER

FOREWARD BY GEORGE L. DAVIS

God's Future for You
by André Butler

Published by HigherLife Development Services, Inc.
400 Fontana Circle
Building 1 – Suite 105
Oviedo, Florida 32765
(407) 563-4806
www.ahigherlife.com

Unless otherwise noted, Scriptures are taken from the King James Version of the Bible.

Scriptures marked AMP are taken from the Amplified® Bible, Copyright © 1954, 1958, 1962, 1964, 1965, 1987 by The Lockman Foundation. Used by permission. (www.lockman.org)

Scriptures marked THE MESSAGE are from The Message. Copyright © 1993. Used by permission of NavPress Publishing Group.

Scriptures marked NLT are from The New Living Translation: Holy Bible. New Living Translation copyright© 1996, 2004, 2007 by Tyndale House Foundation. Used by permission of Tyndale House Publishers Inc., Carol Stream, Illinois 60188. All rights reserved.

Scriptures marked NIV are from THE HOLY BIBLE, NEW INTERNATIONAL VERSION®, NIV® Copyright © 1973, 1978, 1984, 2011 by Biblica, Inc.™ Used by permission. All rights reserved worldwide.

To my Tiffany Diamond and my three little princesses:
Alexis, Angie, and April.

I love you all more than I can express.

TABLE OF CONTENTS

Foreword

Pastor André Butler has been like a brother to me since he was a small child. Since then, I have watched him grow and develop into the great man of God that he is today. He was raised in a godly environment his entire life and called into full-time ministry as a young adult, where he has served faithfully and successfully for many years as a beloved shepherd to a congregation of thousands. He is a devoted husband and father with a loving, happy, healthy marriage and family life, and he is experiencing the "good success" in all aspects of his life that the book of Joshua talks about (Josh. 1:8).

As someone with a wealth of knowledge of the Word of God, a personal life that testifies to the truth and power of it, and a "future" of his own that is even bigger, better, and brighter than the blessed life he currently has, Pastor André is someone whom I would be eager to listen to concerning this subject.

Given the climate of today's society, where we are inundated with death, darkness, deception, destruction, depression, and despair, even those who do not proclaim to be Christians should be interested in reading further. The world is blindly searching in all the wrong places for solutions to these and other problems. The reason they cannot find the answers is because those answers cannot be found anywhere outside of a solid relationship with God. Everybody wants to win and succeed in life. Some people are just on the wrong path or using the wrong navigation system to get to that destination called Victory.

This book is definitely good news for the person who believes there is a real God who is willing and able to make unlikely, even impossible things happen for them personally, not just for "everybody else." This book also serves as a source of hope for anyone who has not come to know as their heavenly Father the loving God who is discussed in this book, who has a great plan and bright future for every one of His children.

I challenge, encourage, even admonish you to go on this journey into your bright future with Pastor André as your tour guide and a loving, trustworthy, heavenly Father leading every step of the way! If you do, I believe it will produce results in your life that far exceed anything you could have asked for or imagined.

George L. Davis
Senior Pastor
Faith Christian Center
Jacksonville, Florida

ACKNOWLEDGMENTS

I would like to give honor to my Lord and Savior, Jesus Christ, who has saved me and given me the honor of helping Him save the world. Also to my parents and sisters, Bishop Keith Butler, Pastor Deborah Butler, Pastor MiChelle Butler, and Minister Kristina Butler. Without all of you, I would not be who I am. I also would like to acknowledge Rev. Kenneth E. Hagin, Rev. Kenneth W. Hagin, Kenneth and Gloria Copeland, and the many other outstanding men and women of God who have taught me the word of faith. I am forever grateful!

When the LORD turned again the captivity of Zion,
we were like them that dream.

Then was our mouth filled with laughter, and our
tongue with singing: then said they among the heathen,
The LORD hath done great things for them.

The LORD hath done great things for us; whereof we are glad.

Turn again our captivity, O LORD, as the streams in the south.

They that sow in tears shall reap in joy.

He that goeth forth and weepeth, bearing precious seed,
shall doubtless come again with rejoicing, bringing his
sheaves with him.

— Psalm 126

Live the Dream

When Tiffany and I found out we were going to have our first child, we couldn't wait for the very first ultrasound so that we could actually see her. The doctor printed out pictures for us of our tiny daughter in her mother's womb. I kept them in my wallet for years, and from time to time I would pull them out and just look at them. In one picture, she had a little hand lifted up like she was praising God. "She's already shouting, 'Hallelujah!'" I told Tiffany.

Each night, Tiffany would read *What to Expect When You're Expecting* and tell me what was happening with our baby, how she was growing, and how God was forming her. We paid a lot of attention to every step of that process because once we found out that Alexis was coming, immediately she became valuable to us. She became the most important person in our lives, outside of Jesus and each other.

If you're a parent, you probably went through the same thing when you found out you were having a child. You thought about what kind of person your son would become, what your daughter was going to do, what their favorite things would be, and about your relationship with them.

That Is How God Feels About You!

God had you on His mind before you were even born. He already loved you. He watched you in your mother's womb. He wrote down things about you. He knew where you were going and who you would be. Most of all, He had a picture in His mind of what your relationship with Him would be like. God had a dream for your life. In the next twenty-eight days, I want to show you that God not only had a dream for your life, but today He still has a dream for your future. He still cares about you, and He still wants you to experience the life He planned for you.

Someone once said, "When I look at my children, I never think about their past, only their potential. This is how God sees us." God has a dream for your future.

"How precious also are thy thoughts unto me, O God! how great is the sum of them! If I should count them, they are more in number than the sand: when I awake, I am still with thee" (Ps. 139:17–18).

God is thinking about you. Not only is He thinking about you, but He's thinking precious thoughts about you. He's not thinking about how you messed up yesterday. He's not thinking about how mad He is because you didn't do something you said you were going to do. He's not thinking about how you messed up six years ago or twenty years ago. No, He's thinking good thoughts about you—precious thoughts— because you are precious to Him. You are so precious to Him that He has numbered the very hairs on your head (see Matthew 10:30 and Luke 12:7). His thoughts about you are so great that the psalmist says, "O God! how great is the sum of them!" (Ps. 139:17). God doesn't just think a good thought about you once a year. He's got precious thoughts going through His mind about you all the time. He's thinking about how much He loves you, how much He values you, and how much He wants to see you live the life He planned for you all along.

And that's what we're going to discover in the next four weeks: God's dream for you. You are going to understand exactly what He had planned for you all along and then learn how to live that dream. You'll see how it will not only impact you but also help you show those around you how they can have the future God wants them to have.

God Has an "Inception" for You in His Mind

Not too long ago, there was a movie called *Inception* about criminals who were trying to implant an idea in somebody's mind. That's what the enemy has been doing to you. He's been implanting ideas in your mind that you're a failure before God, that you'll never understand what God wants you to do, that you're not valuable, and that you're just another number. God wants to do an "inception" of His own. He wants to plant in your mind the dream that He has for you. He wants you to see that you are valuable to Him, that no matter what's happened in the past, His eraser doesn't leave little tiny marks. No, He's wiped away the past. He has a wonderful future for you where you'll do mighty things for Him. If it's been bad in the past, that's just going to make your testimony better in the future.

My goal in this book is to plant something in your mind and in your heart so that you'll "live the dream"—so that you'll live out the story

God has written for your life. If you live the dream that God has for you, you'll love your future, because the bottom line is that God's dream for your life is for you to experience the future He's had for you all along.

Psalm 126:1 tells us, "When the Lord turned again the captivity of Zion, we were like them that dream." God turned it. There was a

> I want to instill in you hope that your future can be all you and God want it to be.

turning point when the captives went from captivity to living as if they were in a dream. If you live God's dream for your life, you're going to see that your life will end up being like a dream.

I want to instill in you hope that your future can be all you and God want it to be. In the next twenty-eight days, you'll see the purpose and plan for your life through God's eyes. You'll see the future He has for you. You'll learn the five elements of that future and how to live them out:

1. How to walk with God
2. How to make real friends
3. How to enjoy your life
4. How to make your mark
5. How to save your world

Although the world's future is bleak, you can enjoy the greatest years of your life as you follow God's plan for your life.

Before you turn the page, I encourage you to make a decision right now to pursue and live God's dream for your life. Remove the word *impossible* from your vocabulary because God didn't call you to live a life limited by impossibilities. He called you to live a life where nothing is impossible to you because you're with Him and He's in you and for you.

Are you ready to learn what happens when you choose to "live the dream"?

Here's how the twenty-eight day challenge works:

Step 1: Buy the book.

Step 2: Keep up with the readings every day.

Step 3: Meet weekly with a small group to discuss the "God's Future for Me" questions at the end of each section.

Step 4: Buy a book for a friend and encourage him or her to take the twenty-eight-day challenge also.

This book covers the five elements of your future and will span the course of four weeks. Small groups are helpful when you are undertaking a challenge like this one. The other people in the group will provide you with the encouragement, motivation, and pats on the back (and sometimes kicks in the pants!) that you'll need to successfully reach the last day of the challenge.

So, let's get started. Let's discover together the future God has for you!

— DAY 1 —

Future

"I am come that they might have life, and that they
might have it more abundantly."

— John 10:10

If you're like the rest of the people on the planet, you want a future that's bright and wonderful and where all your dreams come to pass. At the very least, you want a future that's better than your past. What if I could promise that you can make sure your future is everything you want it to be? What if I could show you how to take your future from a question mark to an exclamation point—so that you can live the "happily ever after" kind of ending you want to have?

That may sound like a surprising guarantee, considering the state of the world around us. Many people are not exactly confident that there's any hope at all for their future. I want you to know that although the world's future is bleak, your future can be wonderful. You can enjoy the greatest years of your life by following God's plan for your life—and in the next four weeks, you will learn how.

**You can enjoy the greatest years
of your life by following
God's plan for your life.**

5

A few years ago, my church conducted a poll among college students asking, "What do you think when you hear the word *future?*" One of the words that showed up repeatedly was *despair.* Other words were *uncertainty, fear, danger,* and even *death.*

Truthfully, if you decide to do things your own way, then those things are in your future. The Bible says that there is a way that seems right to man, but end thereof is death (Prov. 14:12). But if you decide to follow God's plan for your life, if you say, "God, I take my hands off the wheel, and You can drive," you'll find that the future God has for you is far better than any future you could create for yourself.

In Jeremiah 29:11, God made this promise to the nation of Judah while they were in captivity: "For I know the thoughts that I think toward you, saith the LORD, thoughts of peace, and not of evil, to give you an expected end." That promise applies not just to ancient Judah but also to you and me. God is thinking about you, and His thoughts toward you are good. The word *thoughts* in this verse is also translated as "plans." So you could actually say, "God is thinking about His plans for you," and His plans are for peace. Peace does not refer to the absence of war but rather the absence of lack. The word *peace* in Hebrew is *shalom* and it means "safety, happiness, welfare, and prosperity." It ultimately refers to being whole, having nothing missing and nothing broken in your life. If you are whole, then you have no lack. So God's plan for your future is that there is no lack in your body, your finances, your marriage, your career, your relationships, or even your children's prosperity. That is the plan He has for your future.

The verse in Jeremiah goes on to say, "thoughts of peace, not of evil." So many people today mistakenly believe that God is the cause of evil in the world, but Jesus said, "The thief cometh not, but for to steal,

It is not God's plan for you to experience evil, lack, sickness, disease, destruction of your relationships, or losing your job. Those are the enemy's plans for you.

and to kill, and to destroy: I am come that they might have life, and that they might have it more abundantly" (John 10:10). It is not God's plan for you to experience evil, lack, sickness, disease, destruction of your relationships, or losing your job. Those are the enemy's plans for you. Of course, you will sometimes have what the Bible calls the "evil day" (Eph. 6:13), when Satan will attack you, but God's plan for your future is that even in those days you become more than a conqueror through Him who loves you.

In that same passage from Jeremiah, the Lord goes on to say that His plan is "to give you an expected end." The NIV translation says, "I know the plans I have for you . . . plans to prosper you and not to harm you, plans to give you hope and a future." That's the future He has for you.

God's Plan for His People

Throughout the Old and New Testaments, we see examples of people God called and promised a great future. God called Abram at age seventy and told him to leave everything and go to a foreign land. Then God told him His plan for his future: "I will bless you there. I'll make your name great. You'll be the Father of a great nation" (see Genesis 12:1–3). Joseph was about seventeen years old when God revealed to him in a dream that his family would bow down to him and that he would be in a position of authority. God showed Moses that he would deliver Israel out of Egypt. He called a fifteen-year-old shepherd named David to be the next king of Israel and later told David's son Solomon that he would be the richest and wisest man in the world and would have victory over Israel's enemies.

In the New Testament, God called Peter and told him he would be a leader of the early church—in spite of the fact that he denied Jesus three times. God called Paul, one of His fiercest enemies, and promised him a great future, using him to write two-thirds of the New Testament. And what about that babe in a manger? An angel told His mother that God had great and mighty things planned for this child and that he would be the King of kings and the Lord of lords.

God had a future for all these people—and He has a future for you. I can't tell you specifically what that is, of course, but I can give you a big-picture view of what your future will look like if you follow God's path for you: "The path of the just is as the shining light, that shineth more and more unto the perfect day. The way of the wicked is as darkness: they know not at what they stumble. . . . Ponder the path of thy feet, and let all thy ways be established" (Proverbs 4:18–19, 26). This path does not refer to one decision but rather a series of decisions or a lifestyle. God is saying to "ponder the path of your feet"—see which path are you on. One path leads to brightness; the other to darkness. Psalm 115 says that when you are on this path, you will "increase . . . more and more," unto the perfect day (v. 14). That is what it means to be on the path of the just. Job says, "Though thy beginning was small, yet thy latter end should greatly increase" (Job 8:7). That is how God works. You don't always get where you're going overnight, but God promises to increase you more and more each day. Once you get on this path, there is nothing Satan can do to keep you from increasing.

It's time to "ponder" what path you are on. If you determine you are not on the path of the just but rather on your own path, trying to create your own future, you have a life-changing choice to make, which God set before you in Deuteronomy 30:19: "I call heaven and earth to record this day against you, that I have set before you life and death, blessing and cursing: therefore choose life, that both thou and thy seed may live."

Today is your day when the Lord says, "It's time to leave that old life and come to the life that I have for you right now." There are only two choices: life or death. We live in a world that wants to create a gray area, but there is no gray area. God makes it very clear: "I set before you life and death." The life He is talking about is not just physical life, but also spiritual life. He is inviting you to have a relationship with Him where you not only enjoy the benefits of that relationship on this earth but throughout eternity with God in heaven. Death is not just physical death, but ultimately spiritual death—when you spend eternity without God in the Devil's hell. That was never God's plan for your future, but if that is the one you choose, He will honor your choice. He made you a free agent. You can choose to go wherever you want to go.

God sent His Son, Jesus, so that you could have a choice. He is your only hope of getting out of the bleak future that the world offers and stepping into a wonderful future. That is what John 3:16 is all about: "For God so loved the world, that he gave his only begotten Son, that whosoever believeth in him should not perish, but have everlasting life."

Today is your day. You get to decide what kind of future you are going to have. I encourage you to say yes to God. I guarantee that if you do and stay on that path, you are going to enjoy the greatest years of your life.

Walk With God

Enoch walked [in habitual fellowship] with God.

— Genesis 5:22 (AMP)

— DAY 2 —

Friend Request

Abraham…was called the Friend of God.

— James 2:23

More than half a billion people around the world are on Facebook. If Facebook were a country, it would be the third-largest country on the earth. In the world of Facebook, if I want you to become my friend, I'd send you a "friend request." If you accept that, you'd be part of my circle of friends, know what was going on in my life from my viewpoint, and see the pictures I post and my status. I'd be able to direct-message you and chat with you.

What if Jesus had a Facebook page? And what if He sent you a friend request? In a sense, He does and He has! He wants you to see His wall, to know His secrets, to see His pictures, to see life through His viewpoint, and to be part of what He's celebrating. He wants to be able to direct-message you from time to time and chat with you every single day.

So here's my question to you: Will you accept His friend request? Will you let Him be your friend? So many people today are looking for happiness, purpose, and fulfillment—often in the wrong places. If you want to experience God's future for you, then be a friend to God and let Him be a friend to you.

Can that actually happen? How can you be friends with God? Let's look at what He says and examples of people throughout the Bible who were called "friends of God."

In John 15, Jesus spoke to His disciples—the group of men who walked with Him daily—and told them how to be His friends: "Ye are my friends, if ye do whatsoever I command you. Henceforth I call you not servants; for the servant knoweth not what his lord doeth: but I have called you friends; for all things that I have heard of my Father I have made known unto you" (vv. 14–15).

In Genesis 3, God came down and walked in the garden in the cool of the day. Why? Because He wanted to walk with His man, Adam. That showed that Adam was His friend. Abraham was a friend of God (Jas. 2:23). Enoch and Noah both walked with God (Gen. 5:22; 6:9). God spoke with Moses face to face like He would a friend (Ex. 33:11). David was a friend of God (Acts 13:22).

How did these people become friends of God? And how can you? Jesus said, "Ye are my friends, if ye do whatsoever I command you"

Friendship with God is available not just to people in the Bible but to you and me.

(John 15:14). The Message translation puts it this way: "You are my friends when you do the things I command you. I'm no longer calling you servants because servants don't understand what their master is thinking and planning. No, I've named you friends because I've let you in on everything I've heard from the Father."

Friendship with God was not available only to people in the Bible; it is also for you and me. Paul said, "The intimate friendship of the Holy Spirit, be with all of you" (2 Cor. 13:14, THE MESSAGE). The King James Version of this same verse says, "The communion of the Holy Ghost, be with you all." Other versions translate it as "fellowship"—just hanging out. Notice the last few words: "be with you all." So being a friend of God wasn't just for Adam, Abraham, Moses, Peter, or John. God wants to be a friend to you, too.

Rights and Privileges of the Friends of God

As you can imagine, when you respond to God's friend request, you enjoy a lot of benefits because you are maintaining a relationship with Him and interacting with Him on a daily basis. Let's look at some of those benefits.

You experience righteousness, peace, and joy. "For the kingdom of God is not meat and drink; but righteousness, and peace, and joy in the Holy Ghost" (Rom. 14:17). What matters in the kingdom of God is righteousness—you being right with God. The kingdom is about you having peace. That's not the absence of war but the absence of anxiety. It's about you experiencing joy in the Holy Ghost. This joy is a supernatural joy; when you have joy, you can be emotionally happy even when you're going through a difficult time. That's a benefit of being God's friend.

You have an advisor who guides you into all truth. "Howbeit when he, the Spirit of truth, is come, he will guide you into all truth: for he shall not speak of himself; but whatsoever he shall hear, that shall he speak: and he will shew you things to come" (John 16:13). The Message version of this verse says, "When the Friend comes, the Spirit of the Truth, he will take you by the hand and guide you into all the truth there is." That means He shows you the way. If you walk with God, He will be an advisor and counselor to you. The world can only guess at the best decision to make, but you'll know every time.

He delivers you from sin in your life. "If the Son therefore shall make you free, ye shall be free indeed" (John 8:36). Another benefit of walking with God—of responding to His friend request—is that He will be your deliverer. The longer you walk with Him, the more sins from the past you'll shake off. You will be the one God uses to reverse the curse in your family and start a line of blessing and holiness.

He protects you from all evil. Just before Jesus was crucified, He asked His Father, "I pray not that thou shouldest take them out of the world, but that thou shouldest keep them from the evil" (John 17:15). The word *keep* here means "to guard them from injury or harm." He was not only praying for His disciples, but also for everyone who would come after them—that means you and me. "God, I am praying that You guard _____ from the evil one" (fill in your own name here). When you walk with Him, He protects you from all evil.

You have access to the throne of grace in time of need. He says you can come "boldly" to that throne (Heb. 4:16). It's your right and privilege as His friend. There is always grace available to help you, no matter what you face. When you are with God, nothing shall be impossible.

How You Actually Walk With God

Those are the benefits of responding to God's friend request, but how do you actually do that? What does it mean to walk with God? Here are four keys to being God's friend.

1. Put God first. "Delight thyself also in the LORD: and he shall give thee the desires of thine heart" (Ps. 37:4). God is online now, waiting for you to log in. So the first thing you have to do if you want to be God's friend is to put Him first. Throughout the Old Testament, we see Israel putting other things in priority above God, even though He was supposed to be number one in their lives. He called that playing the harlot because He saw His relationship with His people like a marriage. Put God first in your life, and keep Him there.

2. Draw nigh to God. "Draw nigh to God, and he will draw nigh to you" (Jas. 4:8). That is, you draw near to God and then God responds by drawing near to you. Wherever you are becomes the throne room because the King shows up. One of the ways you can draw nigh to God is when you praise and worship Him. Another way is taking the time to pray. Another is to study His Word. David, who was a friend of God, said, "O how I love thy law! It is my meditation all the day" (Ps. 119:97).

3. Don't grieve Him. "If we say that we have fellowship with him, and walk in darkness, we lie, and do not the truth" (1 John 1:6). You can't say, "I'm with God," and purposely walk in sin. Don't live a life that you know is wrong. That's like blocking God on your Twitter page and your Facebook page. You're not letting Him do what He wants to do. You're holding Him back and pushing Him away. You are grieving Him.

4. Care about what God cares about. What makes you friends with your friends is that you have something in common. You care about the same things. If you're a friend of God, you ought to care about what God cares about. When He posts a picture on His Facebook page of somebody lifting their hands because they just got saved, you ought to be excited. The Bible says the angels rejoice when one is saved; you ought to be rejoicing with them.

Jesus has sent you a friend request. How you respond will help determine your future.

— DAY 3 —

Don't Blame God

For we wrestle not against flesh and blood, but against
principalities, against powers, against the rulers of the darkness
of this world, against spiritual wickedness in
high places.

— Ephesians 6:12

*Why do bad things happen to good people? Why does God let
me hurt? Why is life so hard?* We live in a world where terrible things
happen to people all over the world every day—natural disasters,
children dying from hunger, and more. You may have lost a child, been
abused or raped or suffered financial ruin. Why do these terrible things
happen? And who do we blame for them? Many people—believers
and non-believers alike—immediately blame God for these terrible
things. "He's building character in me. He must have needed that child
in heaven. He ____ (fill in the blank)."

Today we are going to settle once and for all that God is not to blame
for these tragic situations or any other. In the process, we will get a
godly perspective on what is going on in our lives and in the world
around us. As long as you blame God for negative things happening,
you are not going to walk as closely with Him as you should—and you
will not enjoy the future He has for you.

In Mark 4, Jesus told a parable about a man sowing seed, which is
the Word of God. Satan snatches the seed that has not taken root.
What is the result? "When affliction or persecution ariseth for the word's
sake, immediately they are offended" (v. 17). This is a parable of God
sowing His Word in our hearts and lives. If God is the one who sent the

Word to you so that it can produce in your life, God will not at the same time send affliction and persecution against you so that the Word won't work. That wouldn't make sense, would it?

In John 10:10, we read that Jesus said, "The thief cometh not, but for to steal, and to kill, and to destroy: I am come that they might have life and that they might have it more abundantly." The thief is the Devil. He is coming to steal from you—your health, your peace of mind, your money, your children, whatever he can take. In fact, his goal is not just to steal, but to kill and destroy. He doesn't just want your body. He wants your soul.

In John 17:15, when Jesus was praying for His disciples and for us, He asked the Father to "keep them from the evil." Why would Jesus ask His Father to protect us from evil if He were doing the evil?

Can you see how we've blamed God all this time for what is the Devil's fault?

In Luke 10:19, He said, "I have given unto you power...over all the power of the enemy: and nothing shall by any means hurt you." Why would He give us authority over evil if He was doing the evil?

Let no man say when he is tempted, I am tempted of God: for God cannot be tempted with evil, neither tempteth he any man....Do not err, my beloved brethren. Every good gift and every perfect gift is from above, and cometh down from the Father of lights, with whom is no variableness, neither shadow of turning.

— James 1:13, 16–17

Can you see how we've blamed God all this time for what is the Devil's fault? We've had the wrong guy on trial. We've put God up on the stand, and we've been trying Him for what He is supposedly doing in our lives, while the real murderer is running loose. A madman is on the loose—a serial killer who is stealing, killing, and destroying. Instead of going after him, we have been shaking our fist at God. If you add a "d" to the word "evil," you get "devil." If you add an "o" to the word "God," you get good. So if it's from God, it's good. If it's evil, it's from the Devil.

God created the earth for mankind. He created it, then He leased it to man, and then He rested. That's why He told man to subdue the earth. So in the garden, when Satan used a serpent against Adam, Adam had the authority to subdue it. He could have said, "Die right now." God could see what was happening but He couldn't just step in because He had leased the earth to Adam and Eve. Adam had to deal with this. Whatever he did was going to determine the atmosphere of this planet until the lease is up. What did Adam do? He handed over the lease to Satan. Satan said it to Jesus when he tried to tempt Him: "All the kingdoms of the world have been delivered to me" (see Luke 4:6). Jesus did not dispute it. Instead, He acknowledged that Satan is the god of this world (see John 12:31; 14:30).

That is the battle that still rages to this day. It is the battle that Paul wrote about when he said we wrestle "against principalities, against powers, against the rulers of the darkness of this world, against spiritual wickedness in high places" (Eph. 6:12).

Can you see that the Devil is the one firing darts at you—not God? The Devil is the one who forms weapons against you to destroy you. God is the one telling you to put the armor on and use your shield so that you can be protected (v. 11). God is good. The Devil is evil. Whatever you're going through, whatever happened to you, whatever is going on right now, whatever the enemy sends against you in the future, don't blame God. Don't fall for that trick. The Bible says that Satan is a great deceiver. That's what he does, and he has deceived so many.

When you blame God for what is going on in your life instead of the Devil, all of the sudden you take a step away from God and miss out on what He really wants you to have—your future. When you should be running to Him for help and comfort, suddenly you're offended by Him and turning away. Blaming God instead of the Devil does something else; it takes all the responsibility for negative things happening in your life out of your hands—because sometimes (let's be honest) you mess up. Sometimes the fault is yours. You made a bad decision and now you're paying the price for it.

Are the Following Statements True or False?

1. "God causes natural disasters, famine, hunger and other tragedies"—true or false? The answer is "false." Look at the book of Job, which is about Satan trying to get Job to curse God: "So went Satan forth from the presence of the LORD, and smote Job with sore boils from the sole of his foot unto his crown" (Job 2:7). Who is the one who made Job sick? Satan.

2. "God causes evil circumstances to teach me something"—true or false? False. God doesn't make you poor or sick or cause a loved one to die in order to teach you something. The one who teaches is the Holy Ghost, not Satan. Jesus says, "The Comforter, which is the Holy Ghost, whom the Father will send in my name, he shall teach you all things" (John 14:26). Sometimes He teaches us through the Word of God, sometimes through other men and women of God, and other times by leading and guiding us. Nowhere in the Word does it say that God uses Satan's tools to teach you His lessons.

3. "God causes evil circumstances to develop your character"— true or false? False. If God sent sickness to you to develop your character or to teach you something, aren't you out of the will of God when you go to the doctor to get rid of the sickness? If He sent financial trouble your way to teach you something or develop your character, then aren't you wrong to get a job? If He sends trouble your way to teach you something or develop your character, aren't you wrong to turn around and go to the many Scriptures where God says, "I will deliver you out of trouble"? And at what point do you know that you learned a lesson and it's all right to ask God to heal you? How do you know your character has matured so that you can say, "All right, God, deliver me"? Do you see how the Devil has twisted your thinking?

4. "God will make the best of a bad situation"—true or false? True. He'll take what was meant for a curse and turn it into a blessing. The enemy will send something against you, and in the middle of it God will make that trouble work for you, but He will not send you trouble

22

in the first place. He simply takes what Satan meant for evil and turns it to good.

This is a very critical day in our twenty-eight-day study because I want you to settle this once and for all: God is not your problem. He is your answer. Will you commit to not blaming God?

— DAY 4 —

Back to the Future

"Don't look back!"
— Genesis 19:17 (THE MESSAGE)

All of us, myself included, can look back at our lives and see areas where we made mistakes and failed. Should we let that keep us from having the future that God intends us to have? No. In fact, you must let go of the past to walk with God into your future. Today we're going to look at a number of people throughout the Bible who looked back at their lives, and we will see how it affected their future.

Lot's Wife

In Genesis 19, we read about the wicked cities of Sodom and Gomorrah. Their sin was so great that God planned to destroy them. There was at least one righteous man in the city, however, named Lot. God planned a rescue operation to get Lot and his immediate family out of the city before He destroyed it. God sent angels to literally pull them out and gave them one rule: "Don't look back."

You know what happened. Lot's wife turned and looked back at the city they were just rescued from (v. 26). The Hebrew for *look back* means "to scan, look intently at, regard with pleasure, favor, or care." This woman didn't just glance back. She looked back with longing, scanning it, looking intently at her old home, missing it. The Bible teaches that Lot was a righteous man, but it never says that his wife was righteous. Because she decided to focus on the sin in her past, she put herself in a position where she had no future.

You can look back at your former lifestyle and learn from your mistakes, but you cannot focus on the sin that you have been delivered from or long for it. If you keep focusing on what you did, it will cost you your future. The "good old days" weren't so good. That's why you left them. There's a reason why you walked away from that sin and lifestyle. It brought about pain, suffering, and destruction.

When God delivered Israel out of Egypt, they were in the wilderness for only a little while before they began to complain about not having enough food. "If only we had died in Egypt," they cried. "At least we had more bread than we could eat." That complaining ultimately cost that generation the future God had for them—going into the Promised Land. They died in that wilderness, and God waited until a new generation grew up before taking them into the promise.

Did you ever notice that the front windshield of your car is much larger than the rearview mirrors? That's because you're supposed to spend most of your time looking forward and not backward. There's a place for looking into your past to learn from it, but if you keep focusing on that past, you're going to put yourself in a position where destruction is in your future. Don't be like the dog returning to its vomit (see Proverbs 26:11). If it's on your mind, it's in your future. You might say it's harmless to think about the former things, but it is very harmful. Whatever you meditate on, eventually you will do. You will start thinking about and longing for the past, and it's not long before the enemy gives you a chance to do more than just think about it. Make the decision, "I'm not even going to touch it in my thought life. I'm not thinking about it anymore. I am done with it." Ask the Holy Spirit to help you keep that commitment, and then move on.

Paul

Who had a past like Paul did? Imagine the horrible crimes he committed against Christians and against Jesus Himself. Paul could have wallowed in self-pity and self-examination and come to the conclusion that he'd done so much wrong that God could never possibly use him. Yet he said, "I obtained mercy" (1 Tim. 1:13). There are two sides to obtaining mercy. First, mercy is offered to you, and second, you receive it. Paul understood that God forgave him so he ought to forgive himself. He understood that Jesus's blood washed away his sins. At the end of his life he said, "I finished this course, and there is laid up for me a crown of righteousness in heaven" (see 2 Timothy 4:7–8). He overcame his past failures and stepped into the future God had for him.

Focusing on your past instead of God's future for you will make you believe you've done so many horrible things that God could never use you. Be like Paul and receive the mercy that God is offering you.

Peter

Peter denied Jesus three times, weeping bitterly when he realized what he had done. He broke his own heart. After Jesus rose again, when all of heaven was rejoicing and all the other apostles were rejoicing, where was Peter? He went back to his old trade of fishing

God hasn't given up on you, so don't you give up on yourself. Receive the mercy He is offering to you.

(see John 21:3). Jesus sat with him and talked with him until he overcame those past failures. And after Jesus left, who stood up and began to lead the church? Who preached on the day of Pentecost and led three thousand people to salvation? Who was so anointed that people brought their sick family members just to get them close to his shadow because they knew they'd be healed? Peter. Peter overcame his past failures and walked into the history-changing future God had for him.

I don't know where you messed up, and I don't need to know. But I am here to tell you that the blood of Jesus washed away all the sins you committed. God hasn't given up on you, so don't you give up on yourself. Receive the mercy He is offering to you. He has a great future for you. God is not in the business of throwing people away. He never does that. Stop rehearsing what happened or wishing you could go back to the past. Don't let your past paralyze you. Let it propel you. As much as you may love God, and as much of the Word that you may know, you are going to mess up again sometime in the future. You are going to miss it sometimes even when you love God. What do you do? Get up. Do not give up on your future, because God hasn't.

"I've got my eye on the goal, where God is beckoning us onward—to Jesus. I'm off and running, and I'm not turning back" (Phil. 3:13–14 THE MESSAGE).

— DAY 5 —

Crazy

For we walk by faith, not by sight.

— 2 Corinthians 5:7

A major part of walking with God is walking by faith. Faith will help you get to the destination you're aiming for. Faith is the clay God uses to create the future you want in your life. The word that is commonly translated as *faith* in the King James Version means a "firm persuasion" or "to be fully persuaded." Faith is total confidence in God and His Word. Faith believes what God says in spite of what can be seen.

That's why faith is not of the head; faith is of the heart. No matter what it looks like to your mind, faith is confidence in your heart that God will do what He said He will do. Paul not only tells you how you *should* live, but he also tells you how you *shouldn't* live: "We walk by faith, not by sight" (2 Cor. 5:7). Don't live your life based on what you can see with your natural eyes. Don't make your decisions based on what you feel.

Your body might be wracked in pain, but faith says, "I'm healed." You can't pay your bills, but faith says, "I'm debt free." Your child is off somewhere on the other side of the country, but faith says, "She will not turn away from God even when she's old." Your head says, "Man, the last thing I need to do in this economy is give," but faith says, "The thing you better do right now is give." Faith takes a position that is completely contrary to what your mind says about the situation and what your eyes are seeing. That's why Proverbs 3:5 says, "Trust in the LORD with all your heart and lean not on your own understanding" (NIV).

29

At some point, you've got to make a decision to either trust in what your mind says or trust in what God says.

Stepping Out of the Boat

In one of the last scenes in the movie *Indiana Jones and the Last Crusade,* Indy is standing so close to the Holy Grail that he can almost taste it, but he has to cross a wide ravine. The ancient book he holds tells him to just take a step, but he knows in his mind that if he does, he'll plummet into the bottomless pit in front of him. Finally, in faith, he takes the first step—and suddenly a path appears that wasn't there a moment ago. That's faith.

Real-life heroes of the faith in the Word of God also did things that seemed plain crazy, but they followed God in obedience because of faith. They walked by faith, not by sight, and we can learn from their example. God called Peter to step out of the boat and onto the water—and it wasn't a calm day, either. The wind and waves were kicking up all around him. Can't you just hear what was going on in Peter's mind? *Wait a minute, Jesus. That's crazy. Nobody has ever walked on water. If I step out of this boat, I'm going to sink.* But he did take the first step—and became the man who walked on water. I believe if Peter did not step out of the boat, he never would have stepped out on the day of Pentecost to preach to three thousand people.

It begins with taking a step. Faith doesn't just hear God's Word; faith acts on God's Word. Hebrews 11 is often called the Faith Hall of Fame because it lists the heroes of the faith God called to do things that must have seemed crazy at the time—but they did them, and for thousands of years people have read about them. Noah built an ark when no one even knew what rain was (v.7). Abraham left everything he knew and set out for another country before God even told him where he was going—and took his entire family with him (v. 8). Then he was ready to sacrifice his only son—the one God gave him, by the way—believing that God would raise him up, even from the dead (vv. 17–18). Moses led two million people through the Red Sea, trusting God that they wouldn't all drown (v. 29). For seven days, Joshua sang and danced his way around the impenetrable walls of a city, expecting them to fall (v. 30). The same two words are at the beginning of each one of these verses: "By faith."

Can it get any crazier than that? This is crazy faith. And it's what God is calling you to if you want the future He has for you. God may call you to a country you've never even been to. He may ask you to give an offering when you don't have enough money for a sandwich. Your body may be wracked with pain, and He may ask you to shout and dance in victory, believing that He's going to heal you. Obeying God will often seem crazy. It's crazy to build an ark. It's crazy to thank God, shout, and dance around city walls, but faith acts on what God said.

You may have read what God said. You may have confessed what God said—but are you acting on it? Maybe you're waiting for a brochure or a calendar or an app for your phone with everything neatly mapped out for you. Or perhaps you're waiting for an Internet site where you can find everything you need to know about where you're going.

You want God to show you what will happen five, ten, or even twenty years down the road. That, unfortunately, is not the way God works—at least not for believers. God expects you to trust Him enough to take the first step (the one He's showing you right now) and to believe

> God expects you to trust Him enough to take the first step (the one He's showing you right now) and to believe He'll work out the details.

He'll work out the details. He expects you to trust Him that the future He has for you is better than any future you can create for yourself. Faith follows God's directions step by step, even when you see only one step at a time. Faith follows God's instructions, even when those instructions seem to be the opposite of what you think they should be—even when they seem to be crazy. Faith trusts God.

Yes, you can always get biblical counsel. Proverbs 24:6 says, "In multitude of counsellors there is safety." You want to surround yourself with people of faith who will encourage you to do what God is calling you to do and to help you make course corrections if need be. That's why you need to have crazy faith friends and pastors who trust God and will encourage you to do what God is calling you to do, even if it makes no sense to the mind. If God is telling you to do something and you have a decision to make, talk to them about it and make sure it is God.

What do you have to lose by believing God? What have you already lost because you did not choose to believe God? How many times could you have walked on water? How many Goliaths could you have flattened? At some point, you have to get to a place where you say, "I'm not just going to hear that Word. I'm going to act on it. I'm going to bet my life on it, and if God doesn't catch me, then that's it." Because that's faith. It seems crazy, but faith says, "I trust You, God, with my future."

— DAY 6 —

I Know My Future

For as Jonas was three days and three nights in the whale's belly; so shall the Son of man be three days and three nights in the heart of the earth.

— Matthew 12:40

The scribes and Pharisees were searching for a sign that Jesus was who He said He was, and He replied by telling them His future. Just as Jonah spent three days and nights in the belly of the fish, Jesus would spend three days in the heart of the earth. We call that hell. He wouldn't stay there, however. He said He'd come out and be victorious. That was His future.

There was a television show a few years ago called *Flash Forward.* Everyone on the planet would black out for two minutes and get a glimpse of their future. Have you ever wondered what your life will look like in six months? Or ten years? Today, I'm going to show you that you really can know your future, just like Jesus knew His. Here are three reasons why I know my future and why you can know yours, too.

I know my future because I know my habits.

Paul told Timothy, "Refuse profane and old wives' fables, and exercise thyself rather unto godliness. For bodily exercise profiteth little: but godliness is profitable unto all things, having promise of the life that now is, and of that which is to come" (1 Tim. 4:7–8). The word *exercise* means "to train." Training your body requires a lot of time, effort, and discipline. It doesn't just happen. God is not talking about your physical body, however, but your spirit—the real you. The Message version of this verse says, "Exercise daily in God—no spiritual flabbiness, please!" Another translation says, "Take the time and trouble to keep yourselves spiritually fit."

Notice Paul says, "Exercise thyself." It's easy to look to the pastor to train you, your mama, your husband, or your wife, but God says, "Train yourself. Do what it takes to be spiritually fit." In basketball, if you want to be a good shooter, you spend hours a day shooting jump shots so that when game time comes, your body just naturally reacts. That's where you want to be spiritually. You train your spiritual muscles so that you can be like Jesus. Many people think that's impossible, but God expects it of you. God wants you to be like Jesus. It's not an option. You do this by developing habits like thanking God, reading His Word, praying in tongues, and being led by the Spirit every day. After a while, you'll not only get spiritually fit, but you'll stay spiritually fit.

"Godliness is profitable unto all things, having promise of the life that now is, and of that which is to come" (v. 8). Godliness is beneficial to you in all things now and in the future. If you train yourself spiritually to operate in godliness, you will be blessed in all areas of your life—family, health, career, finances. You will be enriched in every area of life (see 2 Corinthians 9:11).

Your life right now may not look like a blessing, but if you're training yourself in this way and developing these godly habits, then you know your future. It's just a matter of time. And if you have not developed those habits yet, today is the day to start so that you can have the future that you want.

I know my future because I know my actions.

"The wicked worketh a deceitful work: but to him that soweth righteousness shall be a sure reward" (Prov. 11:18). This is the law of seedtime and harvest: what you plant, you reap. If you plant wicked deeds, that's what you reap. If you sow righteousness, you'll have a strong future. Righteousness refers to deeds of righteousness—things you ultimately do for others. If you encourage other people, pray for them, give to them, and serve them, you are doing what Titus says: "zealous of good works" (Tit. 2:14). You will gain a reward for doing that.

What result do you want? If you've been sowing the wrong kind of seed, you've got some stuff coming back that you don't want. Thank God that He is merciful and you can ask Him for forgiveness, but at least learn from what you've done, and don't continue to sow the wrong kind of seed. If you've been sowing good seed, I've got good news for you. Your future is bright because what you have done is going to come back to you. It may not look like it right now, but it will come to pass in your life. I call it the *boomerang principle*: it will always come back to you. If this is true, then we ought to sow into our future on purpose. Don't just wait until something happens or comes across your path. Instead, actively look for ways to sow into your future.

I know my future because I know my God.

God told Abraham, "You will be the father of many nations. In you all nations of the earth will be blessed" (Gen. 12:2, paraphrased). Abraham could be certain of his future because he knew the God who told him about it. God told David, "You're going to be king." He also revealed Joseph's future to him—that his family was actually going to serve him. Joseph had to hold on to those words all the time he was in slavery; because he knew his God, he knew his future.

The Devil will always try to get you to doubt your future by doubting what God told you—because even he knows he cannot stop your future from happening. When Jesus called Peter to step out of the

The Devil will always try to get you to doubt your future by doubting what God told you.

boat and said, "Come," all Satan could do was watch. He knew about Peter's future, that stepping out onto the water would lead to greater things. The only way to stop that from happening was to get Peter to take his eyes off Jesus and focus on the things that were not true—so that he might sink. And that's when he sank.

Unless Satan can get you to walk away from your future, it's going to happen. He cannot stop it any more than he could sink Peter. Satan already knows you've received your directive to "come." So don't take your eyes off what Jesus told you. Don't take your eyes off Jesus. Who cares what's going on around you? You are walking on the water!

If you know your God, you know your future. "God is not a man, that he should lie" (Num. 23:19). God is talking about His character. "Hath he said, and shall he not do it? or hath he spoken, and shall he not make it good?" (Num. 23:19). Notice the timeline in this Scripture. God said it in the past, and it's going to happen in your future. Right now, you are just sitting in a time where it hasn't happened yet. It may not look like it is going to happen, yet God's Word tells you it will. God Himself will step in and do whatever it takes to make it good.

What has He said to you about your life? Whatever it is, you can count on God to bring it to pass. You can read Scripture after Scripture about what God said about your family, your career, your ministry, and your health. In every single one of those, you can say, "Thank God, that is what my future is going to look like." Why? Because you know your God. If He said it, He will do it. If He spoke it, He will bring it to pass. When it looks like everything is going in the opposite direction, you are in for a great comeback.

You can say, "This is going to be great to watch because I know how God works. It has to end the way He said it's going to end. If that's the case, my days of singing, 'Nobody knows the trouble I've seen' are over." Your days of wallowing in depression because of your situation are over. This is why you can have joy in the midst of a trial, why you can have peace in the middle of the storm, why you can be like David in the middle of the wilderness being chased by Saul and say, "God, You are my God. Early will I seek You. I am chasing hard after You. I'm not offended at You. I'm not backing away from You. I am running to You because I know You will do exactly what You said You will do. I know my future because I know You."

GOD'S FUTURE FOR ME

1. What did you read in our study the past six days that surprised you?

   _____

   _____

   _____

   _____

2. What did you think about your future before you started this study?

   _____

   _____

   _____

   _____

3. How do you think about your future now?

   _____

   _____

   _____

   _____

4. Briefly describe what God is saying to you about your future. This will probably change throughout the next twenty-eight days, but write as much as you know now.

   _____

   _____

   _____

   _____

5. Quote two Scriptures, one from the Old Testament and one from the New Testament, that prove God has a wonderful future for you (and has had it all the time).

   _____

   _____

_____

_____

6. List other verses that got your attention during the past six days.
   Use them as declarations during the next week to remind yourself
   of God's promises to you about your future.

_____

_____

_____

_____

Make Real Friends

A friend loveth at all times, and a brother is born for adversity.

— Proverbs 17:17

— DAY 7 —

You Are Not Alone

And the LORD God said, It is not good that the man
should be alone.

— Genesis 2:18

Remember the Verizon cell phone ads about the network? The premise was that if your phone service was with Verizon, you were part of a network that followed you wherever you went. You were in the network and had all the benefits of being part of it. Other companies use this same principle as a marketing promotion. American Express says, "Membership has its privileges." But this principle applies to something much more critical than your credit-card company or cell-phone service. It also applies to your spiritual walk.

As a pastor, I've found that most churches have a group called *the insiders*—the church within the church—and another called *the outsiders*. I am not referring to a clique or people who have a particular privileged status. I'm talking about their involvement in the ministry and the lives of other Christians. I can tell you there is a drastic difference in the quality of life of those who are in and those who are out.

I'm asking you: Are you part of the network? Are you an insider or an outsider? Are you part of the in-crowd, or have you elected to be a part of the out-crowd? Have you connected with other believers and decided to do life together? Are you enjoying your Christian life like you really should? If you have a desire to enjoy this life that God has given you and at the end of it hear God say, "Well done, good and faithful servant," you're going to have to get in. You have to stop sitting on the sidelines and instead get connected with other believers and walk with them together.

Here is what the Bible says about you. You and other Christians are put together, joined together, built together, members together, heirs together, fitted together, and will be caught up together. It doesn't sound like there's room for any solitary saints, does it? You are the body of Christ. If you cut off any part of the body and leave it on the ground, it will shrivel up and die. Unless it's connected with the body, it cannot fulfill its purpose. The same thing is true concerning you. You need other believers. You need to do life together.

One of the keys to experiencing God's future for you is doing life together with other believers. Notice that I didn't say doing *church* together, but doing *life* together. An old proverb says, "If you want to move fast, go alone, but if you want to move far, go together." Forrest Gump said, "Life is like a box of chocolates," but let me tell you what

> ## The people whom you hang out with, associate with, listen to and connect with have a major impact on how you live your life.

the Bible says: life is about relationships. From Genesis to Revelation, the Bible is not only about your relationship with God, but also about your relationship with other believers, and even unbelievers.

Do not underestimate the power of relationships. There is more here than you realize. The people whom you hang out with, associate with, listen to, and connect with have a major impact on how you live your life. We see this in the early church:

And they continued stedfastly in the apostles' doctrine and fellowship, and in breaking of bread, and in prayers. And fear came upon every soul: and many wonders and signs were done by the apostles. And all that believed were together, and had all things common; and sold their possessions and goods, and parted them to all men, as every man had need. And they, continuing daily with one accord in the temple, and breaking bread from house to house, did eat their meat with gladness and singleness of heart, praising God and having favour with all the people. And the Lord added to the church daily such as should be saved.

— Acts 2:42–47

This is a blueprint of how the local church is supposed to operate. We know the story: three thousand people that day chose to receive Jesus. What a first altar call! But notice it didn't stop there: "They continued stedfastly…in fellowship and in breaking of bread." One translation says they "devoted themselves to the common life of the church." The word *fellowship* means "partnership, participation, social intercourse or benefaction." The phrase *breaking of bread* refers not just to Holy Communion but also going over to somebody's house and eating and having a good time. What was the result of this fellowship? The church grew every single day as more people became part of it.

You Were Created for Community

God created you to live in community with other people. He understands how He made you and what kind of environment you need to be in to reach your potential. If you're a gardener, you know what kind of environment you need to create in order for your plants to grow to their full potential and produce fruit, vegetables, or flowers. God knows the same thing about you, and that is why He set up the church the way He did. His goal is for you to get involved and have community with one another so that you can be happy, holy, and productive. Psalm 133:1 says, "Behold, how good and pleasant it is for brethren to dwell together in unity!" Notice it says dwell together, not visit. Dwell together, live together, hook up, and stay hooked up.

We can go back to Genesis 2—the very beginning—to see what God's plan was when he created man. After He created Adam, He said, "It is not good that the man should be alone" (v. 18). You may immediately say, "That's talking about creating a helpmate for him. God was talking about a woman." That is true, but it wasn't just that Adam needed a woman. He needed somebody as a friend. "But", you might ask, "didn't Adam have God? Didn't God come and walk with him in the cool of the garden?" Yes, God will be your friend, too, but just as there is a God-shaped void in the heart of man that only God can fill, there is also a human-shaped void in the heart of man that God Himself will not fill because He wants us to do life together with other believers.

Americans are among the loneliest people in the world. We live among a lot of people, but we don't connect meaningfully with many of them. In a study on relationships that tracked the lives of seven thousand people over nine years, researchers found that the most isolated people were three times more likely to die than those who had strong relational connections. They found that people who had bad health habits, such as smoking, poor eating habits, obesity, or alcohol use, but who also strong social ties lived significantly longer than people who had great health habits but were isolated. In other words, it is better to eat Twinkies with good friends than to eat broccoli alone.

God's dream for you as a loving Father is that you have the same type of connection with your brothers and sisters in Christ that He has with Jesus and the Holy Ghost. Throughout Scripture, we see Them in community, relationship, and unity. God's dream for you is that you have the same type of relationship not only with Them but with each other. Making real friends and walking in spiritual relationship with other believers is important for you. The enemy's most successful strategy is to isolate you so that he can attack and destroy you. Did you ever notice that sheep are never attacked in herds? Sheep are attacked when they get isolated. And that is true for you, too.

Being part of God's network is also important for the world. Doing life together and connecting with other believers will help believers reach a lost and dying world. Jesus told us how:

"That they all may be one; as thou, Father, art in me and I in thee, that they also may be one in us: that the world may believe that thou hast sent me…that the world may know that thou hast sent me, and hast loved them, as thou hast loved me."

— John 17:21, 23

If we are one, we are doing life together. We are walking in love. The credibility of the Gospel in the eyes of unbelievers is heavily impacted by whether or not they see us doing life together in this way. Christian community is the final apologetic. When a thirsty world sees us living life together as God wants us to, that is when they say, "I want what you have. Tell me about your Jesus."

— DAY 8 —

Face Time

And they, continuing daily with one accord in the temple,
and breaking bread from house to house, did eat their meat
with gladness and singleness of heart.

— Acts 2:46

There's an app for the iPhone called Face Time. If you and I both
have that app, when we call each other, instead of just hearing each
other's voices, I can see your face and you can see mine. It's better
to actually see someone you're talking with, right? When you go to
church services, it's great to get the Word of God, but frankly, the only
interaction you have with other believers on Sunday morning is looking
at the back of their heads. To make new friends, you need face time.
That's why we have faith groups in our church. You might call them
home groups, small groups, cell groups, or care groups. They're an
important part of a believer's life.

We live life among many people, but we don't experience life deeply
with individuals. We even build our homes that way. Years ago, every
home would have a front porch where folks would sit and talk with their
neighbors and even strangers passing by. Not anymore. Most new
homes are purposely designed as walled-in sanctuaries where we can
retreat after dealing with the world all day.[1]

Is that a picture of you? Someone once said, "I've never known a
person who was lonely, unconnected, and with no relationships who
had a meaningful and joy-filled life." If you want to experience the future
God has in mind for you, you can't do it in a vacuum. You have to have

face time with others and allow them into your life. This is why it's so important to do life together:

Two are better than one; because they have a good reward for their labour. For if they fall, the one will lift up his fellow: but woe to him that is alone when he falleth; for he hath not another to help him up. Again, if two lie together, then they have heat: but how can one be warm alone? And if one prevail against him, two shall withstand him; and a threefold cord is not quickly broken.

— *Ecclesiastes 4:9–12*

Verses 10–12 above refer to times when you are in trouble. Face time is critical if you want to get through the difficult times in life. Jackie Robinson was the first black major-league baseball player in history, and he was the victim of racial hatred nearly everywhere he played. Pitchers would throw fastballs at his head, and people in the dugouts and stands threw curses and slurs at him. One day when he was playing at home in Brooklyn, he made several critical errors. Taunts and

> **You need friends like the ones in Luke 5 who broke a hole in the roof and lowered their sick friend on a stretcher right in front of Jesus. Who would do that for you?**

jeers surfaced even from his own fans. Teammate and shortstop Pee Wee Reese looked at what was happening, walked over to Robinson, and placed his arm around his shoulder. He simply stood there until the boos subsided. The gesture spoke eloquently to the crowd more than any other words. Jackie Robinson later said that Reese's arm around his shoulder saved his career.

Who is your Pee Wee Reese? Who are you walking with? I don't mean those you see at church. Who are you walking with on your faith journey? Who are your four crazy faith friends? You need friends like the ones in Luke 5 who broke a hole in the roof and lowered their sick friend on a stretcher right in front of Jesus. Who would do that for you? Your cross can be too heavy to carry alone sometimes. Even Jesus needed a friend to help Him, and Simon was part of God's plan for Jesus in that hour. God has a Simon for you, too.

God Is All About Relationships

God is a relational being. Even the terms He uses—Father, Son, children—show this. How do you get these relationships? We've looked at what happened the day the church exploded from 120 believers to three thousand: "And they, continuing daily with one accord in the temple, and breaking bread from house to house, did eat their meat with gladness and singleness of heart" (Acts 2:46). They met in homes as well as in a larger corporate setting. They needed both. You can worship with the crowd, but you can't connect with one—that happens in a small group. In the Gospels, sometimes Jesus ministered in the temple, and many other times He ministered in homes. In fact, many of the miracles He performed were not in the temple or even in a large group, but in small groups in homes. If you look only at Jesus's public ministry, you miss half of what He did.

Let's study some verses that show the prominence of the house in the early church:

When they were come in, they went up into an upper room, where abode both Peter, and James, and John, and Andrew, Philip, and Thomas, Bartholomew, and Matthew, James the son of Alphaeus, and Simon Zelotes, and Judas the brother of James. These all continued with one accord in prayer and supplication, with the women, and Mary the mother of Jesus, and with his brethren.

— Acts 1:13–14

And daily in the temple, and in every house, they ceased not to teach and preach Jesus Christ.

— Acts 5:42

"I kept back nothing that was profitable unto you, but have shewed

49

you, and have taught you publicly, and from house to house."

— Acts 20:20

Greet Priscilla and Aquila my helpers in Christ Jesus....Likewise greet the church that is in their house.

— Romans 16:3, 5

Aquila and Priscilla salute you much in the Lord, with the church that is in their house.

— 1 Corinthians 16:19

What God established in Acts 2, the early church kept as a part of their lifestyle. Meeting in small groups in the homes of believers was a natural part of their walk.

How Do You Pastor a Church of 100,000?

You do it according to the Word of God. You learn what Jethro told Moses: "You're not doing right by the people trying to do this by yourself" (see Exodus 18:14–23). You equip godly leaders, train them, and have them help you to meet the needs of the people. Fifty years ago, David Yonggi Cho started a church in South Korea with just a few people and some prayer meetings. It grew to three thouand people, and Cho still did all the counseling, visits, and ministering. He ended up in the hospital, and doctors told him he couldn't continue at that pace because his body couldn't take it.

While he was hospitalized, he read the book of Acts, and God taught him how today's church has gotten away from God's original plan, which was to meet from house to house. He incorporated that model into his church, and today it has nearly 800,000 members who meet not only on Sunday mornings but in house churches all over the city.

We've incorporated the same model in our church. I've been to Korea twice to learn from what Cho has done. Having pastored a church that did not emphasize faith groups, as we call them, and having pastored one that does, I can say there's a big difference in the lives of the people when they participate in small groups. Often I can tell without even asking people whether or not they're in a group—just by their life. It's that marked of a difference when someone has devoted themselves, like the early church did in Acts 2, to a home group. I didn't say they visit a home group every once in a while. They are like the early church—steadfast. They connect with other believers. And the fruit in their life shows.

In our church, most of our faith groups meet for 60 minutes twice a month. Your church probably has similar small groups that meet for the same amount of time. Is 120 minutes a month too high a price to pay for the benefits that come from it? The average American watches four hours of TV *a day.* Can you come up with two hours *a month* to experience the spiritual benefits of doing life together? Here are some of those benefits:

- You will experience the presence of God.

- You will make real friends.

- You will receive encouragement.

- You will have support, both spiritual and natural.

- You will experience accelerated spiritual growth.

- You will be held accountable.

- You will have a place to save your world.

I want to encourage you today. Don't just talk about doing life together. Don't make excuses for why you shouldn't or can't do life together. Do life together. Find a small group, and be a faithful part of it. It will bless you abundantly. It's a big part of the amazing future God has planned for you.

— DAY 9 —

Let the Sparks Fly

Iron sharpeneth iron; so a man sharpeneth the countenance of his friend.

— Proverbs 27:17

A hundred years ago, if you wanted to sharpen a sword, you would take another piece of iron and use it to grind and polish your sword, metal to metal. The Bible says that in the same way, a man sharpens his friend. Notice that it doesn't say a CD or a sermon or a Scripture. Of course all these things help you spiritually, but the Word says there

You need godly friends who will not always tell you what you want to hear and who won't be afraid to set you straight.

is something else you need: consistent, transparent relationships with godly friends who will sharpen you. That means there's going to be some friction. When iron sharpens iron, sparks fly. It is not always comfortable. You need godly friends who will not always tell you what you want to hear and who won't be afraid to set you straight. And you need to be that type of friend for someone else.

You Need a Spiritual Partner

Proverbs 17:17 says, "A friend loveth at all times, and a brother is born for adversity." The word *friend* means "close associate." This is not just an acquaintance but someone who is with you when things are good and with you when things are bad. They love you when things are good and love you when things are bad. When everything is coming together, they celebrate with you. And when you break apart into pieces, they are there to put you back together again. When you are going through adversity, they are there with you.

Two are better than one; because they have a good reward for their labour. For if they fall, the one will lift up his fellow; but woe to him that is alone when he falleth; for hath not another to help him up. Again, if two lie together, then they have heat: but how can one be warm alone? And if one prevail against him, two shall withstand him; and a threefold cord is not quickly broken.

— Ecclesiastes 4:9

If you were to fall, is there someone to pick you up? That's what a spiritual partner does for you. My definition of a spiritual partner is someone who can provide support and encouragement to you, someone whom you have invited to help you keep your commitments to Jesus Christ. It's someone you can call up and say, "I messed up," and they will pray for you and help you. And when they mess up, you do the same. Throughout the Bible, we see how God paired up spiritual partners: Paul and Barnabas, Moses and Aaron, and Joshua and Caleb.

Who you choose as your spiritual partner is important: "He that walketh with wise men shall be wise: but a companion of fools shall be destroyed" (Prov. 13:20). Once you decided to receive Jesus, you should have left those who are not living in the way you know you should be living. It doesn't mean you don't ever talk to them or that you're rude to them, but that close relationship has been severed. They are no longer your hanging buddies, no longer your best friends who influence your life. Who you hang with is important. Choose your spiritual partner wisely.

Be Real With Them

Let them ask you the hard questions: "How is your work life? How is your prayer life? Where are you on that path to your future? Are you growing spiritually? Are you witnessing to anybody? How are you doing at home?" I'm not telling you to share all your business, but be real. If something is wrong in your life, be real about that: "Confess your faults one to another, and pray one for another, that ye may be healed" (Jas. 5:16). The word *faults* means "slides, slips." Think about the fault lines in California. Scientists know where the fault lines are, and they monitor them. You need godly friends who know the sin that so easily besets you, who will watch your fault line and help you—friends whom you can be real with. This is transparency. On Sunday mornings, people get used to putting on a church face so that everything looks all right. Thank God for your faith confession, and you should maintain your faith confession, but you cannot get help if nobody knows you are hurting. You need to talk. You need to be real with your spiritual partner. That's when they can help you, believer to believer.

Receive From Them

Put yourself in a position to receive correction from your spiritual friend when they challenge you to do what God has told you to do or to grow spiritually. That's why it's so important to develop a godly friendship with another believer whom you can trust with your spiritual walk. We've already looked at Proverbs 27:17, but if we back up a few verses, we read, "Faithful are the wounds of a friend; but the kisses of an enemy are deceitful" (v. 6). I heard someone say once, "Enemies stab you from behind but friends stab you from the front." They make very clear what the deal is. It may be a wound, but it is a faithful wound, and it will help your life. It will help you grow. Some people want to throw away their friends the minute there is a little friction because they don't agree with them about something or because their friend is challenging them in their sin. If a friend challenges you and says some things that are difficult for you to receive, pray and ask the Holy Spirit to show you if there is truth to it. Pray for a willing and contrite heart to receive difficult words as well as the grace to make changes in your life.

Consider One Another

"Let us consider one another to provoke unto love and to good works" (Heb. 10:24). In a spiritual friendship or partnership, your attention shouldn't be on yourself but on the other person. You don't really have to worry about yourself because you know your attention is on the other person and his is on you. All you have to do is focus on helping the other person. That is how you get a team. That word *provoke* means "to incite to do good." One translation says "to stir up." Focus on sharpening the countenance of your friends.

Observe fully the spiritual life of your brother and sister in Christ. Cain had it wrong when he said, "I am not my brother's keeper." Yes, you are. And when your brother falls, be there for him as he is for you.

Being in this type of spiritual committed relationship takes work. It's not always easy. As an athlete, I have had many a coach who has run me into the ground. I went to practice dreading what would take place. He'd have me running until I felt like I couldn't run any more. I've been to practices where teammates got physically sick because of how hard our coaches worked us. But when time came to play and the other team started wearing down, we were sharpened and ready to play to win.

If you aren't challenged, you won't grow. Whenever I get around Kenneth Copeland and he starts talking about the Word, I almost feel like I am a sinner. "I need to read my Bible more," I tell myself. "What's wrong with me? How did I miss that?" He sharpens me. There is something about being around other believers who are pressing in that helps you press in more yourself. It helps you strive to be like Jesus.

If you don't have a spiritual partner who can sharpen you, iron to iron, I encourage you to ask God to bring one to you.

— DAY 10 —
Let God Heal You

Blessed be God, even the Father of our Lord Jesus Christ, the Father of mercies, and the God of all comfort; who comforteth us in all our tribulation, that we may be able to comfort them which are in any trouble.

— 2 Corinthians 1:3–4

Life is full of surprises, and sometimes those surprises aren't good ones. Maybe you've experienced hurt, betrayal, disappointment, tragedy, heartbreak, or worse. Maybe someone has hurt you deeply. Maybe that person was even a Christian. Hurts from the past can make it difficult to make real friends in the present because even if those terrible events happened years ago, they can still hurt today. Emotional damage took place, and you can't just put a bandage on it to fix it.

I don't know about you, but I don't want to live my life like that. I never considered myself to be an extremely emotional person, but I found out in the last few years that I was wrong about myself. If the right buttons are pushed, I can be a very emotional individual. I've had to learn how to overcome those negative emotions. I don't have it all worked out yet, of course, but I'm working on it because I know what the Word says about it. And that's what we're going to study today. I am going to show you that God wants to comfort you, heal you, and bind up your wounds so that you can fully enjoy authentic, meaningful relationships with other believers.

Paul says that God is "the Father of mercies, and the God of all comfort" (2 Cor. 1:3). The word *comfort* means "solace or consolation."

Paul knew something about tribulations. He was beaten, stoned, shipwrecked, and more, yet he had a testimony that no matter what the trouble was, God's comfort was there as well. If there was trouble, there was comfort; if there was more trouble, there was more comfort. That's the same for you. If there's trouble in your life, there's comfort available. God never leaves you to deal with trouble alone.

Paul said that God comforts you so that you can comfort someone else (v. 4). You've heard the expression, "Hurting people hurt people." We can also say, "Comforted people comfort people." When God heals you of your hurts, He also anoints you to share that comfort with others. The Message translation says it this way: "He comes alongside us when we go through hard times, and before you know it, he brings us alongside someone else who is going through hard times so that we can be there for that person just as God was there for us."

The early church understood this very well because they went through intense persecution (see Acts 8–9). Imagine if one of your deacons or elders was stoned to death in public like Stephen was (see Acts 6–7). Imagine if your fellow church members were dragged from their homes and imprisoned. That, of course, is still going on in many parts of the world such as China, North Korea, the Middle East, and many other places. We have to remember to pray for our brothers and sisters who are paying a high price for the Gospel. We are all part of the body of Christ, and 2 Corinthians 1:3–4 applies to us and to them, whether or not we can see them face to face. God comforts us in our tribulation, "that we may be able to comfort them which are in any trouble."

So how did God fix this in the early church? We know that He stopped some of the persecution by getting the main persecutor saved. Saul the persecutor became Paul the apostle and one of the greatest men to ever walk the planet. "Then had the churches rest throughout all Judaea and Galilee and Samaria, and were edified; and those walking in the fear of the Lord, and in the comfort of the Holy Ghost, were multiplied" (Acts 9:31). The church expanded by leaps and bounds. One of the elements that helped bring about this great move of God was the comfort of the Holy Ghost. It wasn't until they were healed that they were able to go and help God heal the world. If God can do it for them, He can do it for you and for those around you.

A lot of Christians today are like the man in the story that Jesus told about the good Samaritan. A man was lying on the side of the road, beaten and attacked by criminals who stole everything he had and beat him within an inch of his life. Then they just left him on the side of the road to die. A priest came by and didn't help him. A Levite came by and didn't help. A Samaritan came by and not only helped him, but paid for his stay and told the innkeeper that if the man needed anything, he would pay for it. This man lying by the side of the road is where a lot of Christians are today—not physically, but emotionally and spiritually. They've suffered horrible experiences and are near death— yet too many people are walking right on by them. They may have issues of their own that they're dealing with.

God sends us good Samaritans in our time of need. As we're going to see in the coming weeks, He needs us to be friends to those who are hurting and dying in this world. God comforts us and makes us whole—and He wants us to turn around and do the same for others. He not only wants us to be better, but He wants us to go find our brother or sister who is in the same situation and help them to be made whole as well. "He comes alongside of us when we go through hard times and before you know it He brings us alongside someone else who is going through hard times so that we can be there for that person just as God was there for us" (2 Cor. 1:4, 5 THE MESSAGE).

How Do You Let God Heal You?

God wants to heal you—but you have to let Him. How do you do that? Here are four things you must do in order to let God heal you.

1. Encourage yourself. When David and his mighty men came back from battle one day to find their enemies had raided their homes and

God wants to heal you—
but you have to let Him.

taken their wives and children, "David was greatly distressed; for the people spake of stoning him…but David encouraged himself in the LORD his God" (1 Sam. 30:6). David was the perfect candidate for a big pity banquet—not a pity party, but a banquet. Instead, he made a decision to encourage himself in the Lord by spending time with God in praise, worship, and prayer. That's when God gave him a battle plan and they successfully rescued all the women and children who had been taken captive.

2. Believe for supernatural comfort. Ask God for His comfort, believing you will receive it right then (despite how you may feel) and thanking God for it continually. Faith is total confidence in God and His Word. I like to look at that as 100 percent confidence—not 90 percent, not 80 percent, but 100 percent confidence in what God has said. This is in spite of what you may see. That's why the Bible says we walk by faith and not by sight. You not only have to believe that God is able to comfort you, but then you must also receive that comfort in faith.

3. You must forgive. Mark 11:25 says, "And when ye stand praying, forgive." Your prayer is not going to be answered or even heard unless you make a decision to forgive. Let it go. Pardon the person who hurt you. If you don't forgive, your Father in heaven can't forgive you. To resist forgiving is to resist forgiveness.

4. Move forward. David committed a grievous sin by sleeping with Bathsheba and then trying to cover it up. When God said that the child born from that relationship would die, David prayed and fasted that it wouldn't happen, but it did. How did David react? "David arose from the earth, and washed, and anointed himself, and changed his apparel, and came into the house of the LORD, and worshipped: then he came to his own house; and when he required, they set bread before him, and he did eat" (2 Sam. 12:20). David decided it was time to move forward. Notice the end result: "David comforted Bathsheba" (v. 24). He repented of his sin, married her, and God blessed them with a son named Solomon, who also became a great king.

At some point you have to get up and get past what has happened. You have a future that God wants you to live with your brothers and sisters in Christ. Let God comfort you and heal you from your past hurts. Then enjoy the wonderful, meaningful relationships with other believers that God wants you to have in your life.

– DAY II –

Unity

And he gave some, apostles; and some, prophets; and some, evangelists; and some, pastors and teachers; for the perfecting of the saints, for the work of the ministry, for the edifying of the body of Christ: till we all come in the unity of the faith.

— Ephesians 4:11–13

Unity among believers who do life together and have godly friendships is God's ultimate plan and master key for us to win the world to Him. God's will is for the church, the body of Christ, to be unified, but how are all Christians, who are from different backgrounds with different ideas, supposed to be unified? Unity occurs when we grow up spiritually and walk in love with our brothers and sisters in the Lord. They may do things we do not like, get on our nerves, or even stab us in the back, but when we love them as Christ loved us, we can remain united. Christianity is supposed to bring about unity:

For by one Spirit are we all baptized into one body, whether we be Jews or Gentiles, whether we be bond or free; and have been all made to drink into one Spirit. For the body is not one member, but many.... That there should be no schism in the body; but that the members should have the same care for one another. And whether one member suffer, all the members suffer with it; or one member be honored, all the members rejoice with it. Now ye are the body of Christ, and members in particular

— 1 Corinthians 12:13–14, 25–27

Paul used the word *one* three times in these verses to emphasize that although there are many members in the body of Christ, there is only one body. Just as your natural body consists of many parts, the body of Christ has many parts; just as you have only one body, there is only one body of Christ. When one part of your natural body fights against another part, your body can no longer function normally. Likewise, the body of Christ cannot survive when its members fight against another. The body of Christ is supposed to operate as one. How can that happen when there is so much division? "The members should have the same care one for another" (v. 25). When we truly care for one another as Jesus commanded, we will not fight each other.

Hearts Knit Together as One

Paul prayed that the hearts of his brothers and sisters be comforted and knit together in love (see Colossians 2:1–2). When hearts are knit together, they operate as one. As Christians, we should be known for our unity. Isn't that what defines a gang? Gang members warn, "Don't mess with so-and-so or you'll have to answer to the whole gang." If members of a gang get into an argument, they fight behind closed doors. When they're in public, however, they put forth a united front. The body of Christ should be one big Holy Ghost gang, united when we go before the world. If Satan attacks one of us, he should have to deal with all of us. Unfortunately, when people hear the words "body of Christ," they automatically think about a splintered group of people that is spread everywhere, but God's original plan was for people to see one united body all over the world.

Before He was crucified, Jesus prayed for the eleven disciples at the table with Him: "Neither pray I for these alone, but for them also which

Don't miss that! God loves you just
as much as He loves Jesus.

62

shall believe on me through their word; that they all may be one; as thou, Father, art in me and I in thee, that they also may be one in us: that the world may believe that thou hast sent me" (John 17:20–21). If you are a believer, you are one of the people for whom Jesus prayed more than two thousand years ago.

Why is it so important for us to be one? "That the world may believe that thou hast sent me" (John 17:21). Our unity will cause the world to believe in God and His Son, Jesus Christ. Jesus prayed for our unity five times in that prayer. He knew our unity would be evidence to the world that He was sent by the Father who loves them as much as He loves Jesus. Don't miss that! God loves you just as much as He loves Jesus.

Presenting a Unified Front

If you're a parent, you know that one of a child's favorite strategies is to divide the parents. She asks Mama for something and Mama says no. She then goes to Daddy and he says yes. Then the parents get into a big fight in front of the child. Parents must always represent a unified front to their children. If there is something to be discussed, parents should discuss it first behind closed doors and present a unified parental front when they talk to the children. The Bible teaches believers to do likewise. Believers are not to take one another to a court of law. Believers are supposed to resolve their conflicts with other believers, not before unbelievers (see 1 Corinthians 6:1–8).

A unified front means more souls will be saved (see Acts 6). A gang that is always at each others' throats is easily defeated. Sadly, that is what has happened to the body of Christ. We have been so busy fighting over issues, such as whether baptism means to sprinkle or submerge, that we have failed to love one another, and our division allows Satan to come in and destroy young believers. We must walk in love toward one another so that the will of God can be accomplished and we can reach the lost for Jesus.

Paul tells us what to do when fellow believers get on our nerves: "forbearing one another in love; endeavouring to keep the unity of the Spirit in the bond of peace" (Eph. 4:2–3). *Forbear* means "to put up with" and *endeavour* means "to keep trying to live in the unity of the

Spirit." God is calling you to be humble, meek, and longsuffering with your brother so that you can keep the unity.

"If it be possible, as much as lieth in you, live peaceably with all men" (Rom. 12:18). Do whatever is necessary to keep the peace. This also applies to our church bodies; as a church, we should be of "one accord, of one mind" (Phil. 2:2). That is what a church vision articulates. That is why conflict over a church's vision is so detrimental. If God called you to a church, then He called you to help bring its vision to reality. If He did not call you there, then ask Him to lead you to a place where you can be likeminded, have the same love, and be of one accord with the members of the church and the vision He has set forth for the church.

What happens when we are in one accord? In Acts 2, the Holy Ghost showed up when the believers were in one accord and the whole world knew about it. The universal church was started because a group of men were in one accord. We need to operate in love because we need to be unified—one body, one Spirit, one Lord, one faith, one baptism, and one God (see Ephesians 4:4–6)—so that we can present a united front to the world.

Behold, how good and how pleasant it is for brethren to dwell together in unity! It is like the precious ointment upon the head, that ran down upon the beard, even Aaron's beard: that went down to the skirts of his garments; as the dew of Hermon, and as the dew that descended upon the mountains of Zion: for there the LORD commanded the blessing, even life for evermore.
—Psalm 133:1–3

The unity of the early church enabled them to reach a huge portion of the known world in a relatively short amount of time. Unity begins not with millions but with the ones around us. Ask God to help you be unified with the believers He has put in your midst—your friends, family, faith group, and church.

GOD'S FUTURE FOR ME

1. What did you read in this section that was new or surprising to you?

   _____

   _____

   _____

   _____

2. Why are godly friendships an important part of walking in God's future for you?

   _____

   _____

   _____

   _____

3. At the end of the last section, you wrote your understanding of what God's future for you is. Has it changed? Write your latest understanding of it.

   _____

   _____

   _____

   _____

4. What areas from your past does God need to heal so that you can move on to your future?

   _____

   _____

   _____

   _____

5. Quote two Scriptures, one from the Old Testament and one from the New Testament, that show how important unity is to God.

   _____

   _____

_____

_____

6. List the verses that God has quickened to you during this section. Use them as declarations during the next week to remind yourself of God's promises to you about your future.

_____

_____

_____

_____

Enjoy Your Life

If they obey and serve him, they shall spend their days in prosperity,
and their years in pleasures.

— Job 36:11

— DAY 12 —

Enjoy!

Let them shout for joy and be glad, that favour my righteous
cause: yea, let them say continually, let the LORD be magnified,
which hath pleasure in the prosperity of his servant.

— Psalm 35:27

Part of God's future for you is enjoying your life today, and that's what
we're going to focus on in this section.

When you first read the psalm quoted above, it seems like one of
David's typical moments of praising God. It's only when you back up a
few verses that you find out he was facing his enemies and was really
asking God to give him victory. One translation says, "Let all who want
me to win be happy and joyful." What is going to cause them to be
happy and joyful? When God steps into the situation and gives them
victory.

When David says the Lord takes pleasure in the prosperity of his
servant, the word *pleasure* means "to delight in." Another word we
might use today is *enjoy*. So God delights in and enjoys the prosperity

God takes pleasure in and

enjoys it when everything is

right with us.

of his servant. *Prosperity* here means "safe, well, happy, welfare." The Hebrew word that it comes from means "wholeness, to have nothing broken and nothing missing." It means that everything is all right. So God takes pleasure in and enjoys it when everything is right with us.

One of the fruits of the Spirit is joy, and it became a part of your spiritual DNA when you received Jesus as Lord of your life. The Bible refers to it as His joy in you (see John 15:11).You can stir up that kind of joy any time you need it. The Bible also talks about another kind of joy: "Ask, and ye shall receive, that your joy may be full" (John 16:24). This joy is simply your emotional happiness. It's the type of joy you experience when you receive from God the blessings you asked of Him. This verse from John shows us that God wants you to have this kind of joy. You could say He wants you to enjoy your life. In fact, you could say that God's dream for your life is that you enjoy your life. When you enjoy your life, God is also enjoying your life. He's pleased. He's having fun. As we're going to study in the coming days, God wants to bless His people, and He wants you to live your life being a blessing to others.

When God created Adam and Eve, there was no great commission. There was no one for them to preach to. God did not create them for that mission. God created them so that they could enjoy fellowshipping with Him and so that they could enjoy their life. God put all the things on the earth so that they could enjoy their life. When sin entered the world, the enemy began his mission to steal, kill and destroy, but the Father sent Jesus so that you could enjoy abundant life (see John 10:10). Because of Jesus, you can enjoy life to the full, which is what He meant for Adam and Eve to do in the first place.

"O that there were such an heart in them, that they would fear me, and keep all my commandments always, that it might be well with them, and with their children for ever!" (Deut. 5:29). Holiness comes before happiness. That means fearing God and doing what is right in his sight. This is one of the reasons God gave His commandments. If you follow His commands, you will be holy, and the result you get will cause you to be happy. It's the exact opposite of sin. Whatever pleasure sin may give you is temporary, and when it is all said and done, if you add up everything, you end up losing more than you gained.

God's dream for your life is that you enjoy it. Here are some of the many Scriptures throughout the Word of God that show you that is His plan:

- "The fear of the LORD tendeth to life: and he that hath it shall abide satisfied; he shall not be visited with evil" (Prov. 19:23). The fear of the Lord is doing what is right in His sight, or holiness. When you fear the Lord, it leads to life and satisfaction. You won't have any unexpected visits from evil.

- "If they obey and serve him they shall spend their days in prosperity, and their years in pleasures" (Job 36:11). The word *pleasure* means "delightful or sweet." So when you obey God, you will live a life that is delightful and sweet. You will enjoy life.

- "Trust in the LORD, and do good; so shalt thou dwell in the land, and verily thou shalt be fed. Delight thyself also in the LORD: and he shall give thee the desires of thine heart" (Ps. 37:3–4). This is a promise. Notice that David said "desires"—plural. The New Living Translation says "your heart's desires." God didn't tell you to live for the desires of your heart. He said to live for God, but while you do, one of the perks and benefits that come from delighting in and walking with God is that He will give you the desires of your heart. Somewhere in the future is a day marked on God's calendar that He is looking forward to seeing you celebrate because you have received the desires of your heart.

There are many other Scriptures that show God's dream for your future is that you enjoy life (see Proverbs 10:24; Mark 11:24; John 15:7; 16:24). Yes, you're going to have to fight the enemy. Yes, he is going to attack you. Yes, you are going to have days when it doesn't seem like it's going well, but God's will is that you enjoy your life and that whatever your situation, God will turn it around for you.

Three Keys

Here are three keys to making sure you enjoy your life and future. You already know the first one—the verses we just read from Psalm 37. You have a choice. You can choose to delight in the Lord or you can choose to not delight in the Lord. If you didn't have a choice, He would just tell you to do it. He says to trust in Him, do good, have faith,

71

and pursue holiness, but notice that is not enough—He also says you must delight yourself in Him. You must love God with all your soul and all your might.

The second key to enjoying your life is to release your faith: "For verily I say unto you, That whosoever shall say unto this mountain, Be thou removed, and be thou cast into the sea; and shall not doubt in his heart, but shall believe that those things which he saith shall come to pass; he shall have whatsoever he saith" (Mark 11:23). That is the authority God has given you. You can tell a mountain to get in the sea; you can tell a sickness to get away from you; you can tell money to come to you. Whatever you bind will be bound; whatever you loose will be loosed. You can resist the Devil and he will flee from you. All these things are done by releasing your faith through words. You can believe God all you want, but you still have to say something. Faith is voice activated. Satan's ploy is to keep your mouth closed or to keep you saying the wrong thing because fear is voice activated too.

The third key is to be led by the Holy Ghost and patient in receiving. He knows when you need to move forward and when you need to wait. Learn to be led by Him, and wait for His perfect timing. Just because God wants you to have a mate doesn't mean you grab the first knucklehead that comes across your path. So many people end up with Bozo when they wanted to have Boaz. Just because God wants you to have a nice house doesn't mean you go buy it today. Part of enjoying God's future is learning how to hear His voice and move in His timing.

God wants you to enjoy life, and keeping these three keys in mind each day will help you experience the future He has in mind for you.

— DAY 13 —

The Rich Life

For ye know the grace of our Lord Jesus Christ, that, though he was rich, yet for your sakes he became poor, that ye through his poverty might be rich.

— 2 Corinthians 8:9

If you're a parent, you want your children to be blessed in their lives. You want them to have great careers and make a lot of money so that they're financially secure. And you want them to marry the right person and have a great marriage. We could sum it up by saying you just want them to be happy. At the same time you also expect certain things of them. You expect them to pay attention in school, to do the work, and to act like you've taught them to act, because you know if they do, it's going to help them get the results you want to see in their life.

God wants this result in our lives too, and He expects us to pay attention. He expects us to live right so that we can have the rich life He desires us to have. The topic for today could be "The Lifestyle of the Rich and Righteous." Notice I didn't say "lifestyles." We'll talk more about that in a moment. First I want to discuss whether or not God wants us to be blessed and to be rich.

Can you be rich and righteous at the same time? Most of the church today would say, "No, you can't." To most of the body of Christ, rich means wicked. Poor means righteous. So if they see a righteous rich man, they don't know how to handle it. Many born-again Christians who love God really believe that you can't be rich and righteous at the same time.

That's not what the Bible says, as you can see in today's Scripture verse. It clearly says that Jesus paid a price so that you might be rich. This is not just rich financially, but rich in every area of your life. You know what that price was. He went to the cross, became sin for you, became sick for you, became poor for you, and became a curse for you so that you could be rich. Hebrews 2:14 says that Jesus, through death, defeated the one who had power of death. Through death, Jesus delivered you so that you might be rich in every area of your life. He did what He did so that you might be rich.

This is about much more than just money. There are many areas where He wants you to be rich.

For too many years, Christians based their lives and their preaching on the wrong belief that you cannot be rich and righteous at the same time. As a result, the righteous have been anything but rich, while they've been following the richest entity in the universe, the God of extravagance, the God who says, "I will give good things to my children," the God who owns all the silver and the gold and the cattle on a thousand hills, the God who has created prosperity for them.

This is about much more than just money. There are many areas where He wants you to be rich. Here are seven of them.

1. Rich spiritually. God wants you to be rich spiritually and, indeed, because you have Jesus, you *are* rich spiritually. God wants you to be rich in good works, rich in giving, rich in love, rich in judgment, rich in utterance—that you be a mature Christian who indeed lives like Jesus. When you do that, you'll be rich in heaven. You'll make sure you have heavenly treasure waiting for you when you arrive. True richness begins with receiving Jesus, and the first area God wants you rich is spiritually.

Being rich in God is about much more than just money. God gives us a picture of a body of believers who were rich financially but not in other ways—the church of Laodicea in the book of Revelation: "Because thou sayest, I am rich, and increased with goods, and have need of nothing; and knowest not that thou art wretched, and miserable, and poor, and blind, and naked" (Rev. 3:17). The issue wasn't their prosperity; it was that they lost their focus and were not following after God. For them, prosperity was the goal. They were rich in their outward life, but they were poor inwardly. They were poor spiritually. They were rich, but they weren't righteous.

Ultimately, that's what the lifestyle of the rich and the righteous is. It's a lifestyle where you live like Jesus did. Jesus was a rich and righteous man, and it started with being rich spiritually. That's God's will for you, that you be rich spiritually. If you skip this step, you can forget about the rest of what we're going to talk about.

2. Rich in your body. God's will is that you be rich in your body. He wants you to walk in health. That is His will. God provided that for you when He went to the cross and bore your sicknesses and your pains.

3. Rich emotionally. He wants you rich emotionally. God wants you comforted and full of joy. He wants you happy.

4. Rich mentally. He wants you rich mentally, to abound in knowledge, to be even ten times smarter than the unbeliever.

5. Rich in your relationships. It is God's will that you be rich in your relationships. God wants your marriage to be so rich that you're drunk in love with your spouse. God wants your children to be mighty seeds who cause you to be glad parents because of what God has done in their lives and how they've enriched your lives.

6. Rich financially. Proverbs 10:22 says the blessing of the Lord makes you rich financially. God gives His blessing and His power to give wealth to those who serve Him, so that they can be rich financially. The liberal soul, the giving person, will be made rich (see Proverbs 11:25).

7. Rich professionally. God wants you rich professionally. He wants you to prosper in everything you put your hand to. He wants you to enjoy promotion after promotion, to be at the top of your field, blessed above and more productive than the people of this world.

The Narrow Gate

If God wants you rich and righteous, it makes sense that He would show you how to make that happen—and He does:

"Enter ye in at the strait gate: for wide is the gate, and broad is the way, that leadeth to destruction, and many there be which go in thereat: Because strait is the gate, and narrow is the way, which leadeth unto life, and few there be that find it."

— *Matthew 7:13–14*

A straight gate is a narrow gate. So Jesus is saying that the way to destruction is wide, but the gate to life is narrow and the path to it is narrow.

One of our daughters once had a playhouse in the backyard. It's a princess castle because Alexis is a girly-girl. I asked my wife, "Is it normal for a child at age four to be so excited about what she's going to wear tomorrow?" I don't think she's ever going to touch a basketball. Lord, how did You do this to us? She just loved that kind of girl stuff, so she had a princess castle and always wanted Daddy to get in. To get in that castle, I had to contort my body. I had to duck down to get in there. It took everything I could do to get in that castle, and once I got in, I didn't get out quickly.

Living the lifestyle of the "rich and righteous" is like that. The gate is narrow and is going to require you to get down on your knees to enter—to receive Jesus and live for Him. Anything outside this lifestyle is the broad way, the way of the wicked. God wants you to be rich and righteous as part of the future He has for you, so you have to stay right on track with what He has for you to do.

— DAY 14 —

Get It to Give It

You will be enriched in every way so that you can always be
generous. And when we take your gifts to those who need them,
they will thank God.

— 2 Corinthians 9:11, NLT

As I'm writing this book, the world is in the midst of a serious
financial crisis. There's a credit crisis, banks are failing, and people are
losing jobs, their homes, and their investments. I believe you're like me,
and you don't want this recession to have any impact on your financial
life. You want to be "recession proof," which is sort of like wearing a
bulletproof vest. It doesn't mean you won't get shot at, but you'll get
back up again. And when you take off that vest, it's as if you were
never shot in the first place.

God's financial system works for you when you focus on the needs
of others rather than your own. Matthew 6:33 teaches us to "seek
first the kingdom of God" and then "all these things will be added to
you." God's ultimate goal for your financial life isn't just that you receive

**God's financial system works for you
when you focus on the needs of others
rather than your own.**

abundantly but that you give abundantly. God's plan for your life is that you be a generous giver—someone who is so abundantly blessed that you are able to give abundantly for God's purposes. Jesus said, "It is more blessed to give than to receive" (Acts 20:35).

God wants you going through life experiencing the superior joy that comes from giving, and that is one of the reasons why He wants to get abundance to you. Even more importantly, He is thinking of those who are without in this life, especially those without Him, who will benefit from your generosity. God understands that for you to be able to give abundantly, you must receive abundantly. You must get it to give it. One of my desires is to get to a place financially where I can give $1 million a year for God's purposes. My goal is to give abundantly, not just receive abundantly for my own purposes. And when—not if—the time comes that I am receiving from God on that level, it will be vitally important that I remember the purpose it came into my life: so that I can give generously.

Whatever God has given you, some of it is in your hands simply for you to give to His purposes. Remembering the purpose for the money God has given you is an important step in lining up with God's system. It's when God knows that you truly understand this principle that He will trust you with more. In this time of recession, stop focusing on your financial needs and look around for someone you can help with whatever God has placed in your hands. Doing just that will position you to get even more so that you can give more in the days to come. When Paul said his final farewell to the elders at Ephesus, he left them with these words:

"You yourselves know that these hands of mine have supplied my own needs and the needs of my companions. In everything I did, I showed you that by this kind of hard work we must help the weak, remembering the words the Lord Jesus himself said: 'It is more blessed to give than to receive.'"

— Acts 20:34–35 (NIV)

When Paul would go into new areas to preach the Gospel, he purposely would not take offerings. It wasn't because he didn't have a right to do so, but he felt it might hinder the message to ask for an offering from people who knew little to nothing about Jesus yet. Instead, he supplied his own needs and said this was the way to help the weak and those unable to provide for themselves. Paul "got it to give it." Ephesians 4:28 reveals that we should do the same. We shouldn't work for a living; we should work for a giving.

What did God promise Abraham when He made a covenant with him? "I will make you into a great nation, and I will bless you; I will make your name great, and you will be a blessing" (Gen. 12:1–2, NIV). God promised Abraham he would be a blessing to other people. That was Abraham's call. A lot of folks go to work so they can smoke it, drink it, or shoot up with it because they value that high more than anything. I'm here to tell you that we ought to seek a spiritual high. Paul talked about the house of Stephanus and how they addicted themselves to ministering to the saints (see 1 Corinthians 16:15). We should so look forward to the high of giving that we'll do whatever God tells us to get it so that we can give it.

The widow in 1 Kings 17 was about to cook a last meal for herself and her son when God sent a prophet to her, asking for a little bread and water. She stepped out in faith and gave. God performed a miracle, and there was enough flour and oil to eat for days. How did it start? When she got her mind off "getting" and got it onto "giving." That's how the kingdom of God works.

Paul told the church in Corinth, "God is able to bless you abundantly, so that in all things at all times, having all that you need, you will abound in every good work" (2 Cor. 9:8, NIV).The Amplified Bible shares that you will get to the place where you have so much that you "require no aid," which means you don't need to get a loan to buy a car or a house. You live debt free and actually have an abundance besides that. "You will be enriched in every way so that you can be generous on every occasion" (v. 11, paraphrased).

Many believers can quote Luke 6:38 about our abundance being "pressed down, and shaken together, and running over," but the whole point of that verse is the very first word: "Give." There are so many Scriptures that talk about getting it to give it: "He that hath a bountiful eye shall be blessed" (Prov. 22:9); "There is that scattereth, yet increaseth" (Prov. 11: 24).

The world says, "You're in a recession. The last thing you need to do is give." But God says, "If you want increase through Me, then you need to be the person who scatters." God wants you in money ministry not just to meet peoples' physical needs; He wants you to give so that people can receive Jesus as Lord of their life and have eternal life. We don't like to think about it, but there is a connection between money and ministry. It may not seem spiritual, but it is absolutely true. The main purpose for God putting money into your hands is to help Him make sure that every person on this planet gets to hear the Gospel as many times and in as many ways as they need so that they will see the truth and have a chance to receive Jesus.

God has no problem with you driving a nice car or having a nice house as long as you are living to give. Jesus told a story about a rich man who had a huge harvest. He wanted to build bigger and better barns and just store things up and kick up his feet. God said, "You fool, you're going to die tonight. Then what's going to happen with your money?" (Luke 12:20, paraphrased). That is the danger of being rich in this world and laying up treasure for yourself instead of being rich toward God. Jesus said to lay up treasures for yourself in heaven (see Matthew 6:20). At the end of your days, you want to hear Him say, "Well done, good and faithful servant. Enter into the joy of the Lord."

Get it to give it.

— DAY 15 —

The Prosperous Touch

As long as he sought the LORD, God made him to prosper.
— 2 Chronicles 26:5

A mythical king named Midas was the richest person on the earth, yet he desired even more gold and even more money. He got his wish—but his excitement quickly turned to horror because everything he touched turned to gold: his food, his clothes, and even his daughter. He learned that the Midas Touch was more of a curse than a blessing because there is more to life than money.

The Midas Touch is a myth, but there are real people throughout the Word of God who had what I call the Prosperous Touch. King Uzziah was one of them (see 2 Chronicles 26:1–5). The Bible says as long as King Uzziah sought the Lord—not a career, women, money, power, or prestige—God prospered him. Everything he put his hands to prospered, and he had the longest reign of any king in Israel, even David. That tells me that God is in the business of making His people prosper!

Prosperity is all over the Bible. It is rare to find a righteous man in Scripture whom God did not make mega-rich. Abraham, Isaac, Jacob, Joseph, David, Job, Solomon, Uzziah, Hezekiah, Jesus—God made all of them rich. That may go against your tradition, but it's in the Word of God. Having the Prosperous Touch is not something reserved only for kings or Bible heroes. You as a believer can prosper. Everything you put your hands to can prosper. In fact, it *should* prosper! The word *prosper* means "to succeed or be successful, to grow or increase, to

81

thrive and to make gain, as to prosper in business." Let's look at some of the indicators of the Prosperous Touch that we find in the Word.

You Prosper in All You Do

In Deuteronomy 28, God outlined His covenant with us and specified our responsibilities in order to receive His blessing. The word *blessing* in this chapter means "endowment or anointing." God did not say *a blessing* or *blessings*; He was not referring to a house, car, or new dress. He said *the blessing*, referring to an endowed power for prosperity and success. In other words, it is an anointing to prosper.

God wants you to prosper in
all that you do.

God promised, "This anointing will come on you so that you can succeed." He further explained that this blessing would manifest "in thy storehouses, and in all that thou settest thine hand unto" (v. 8). The word *all* means everything! God says, "If you give Me total obedience, I will cause the blessing to come on you in all that you set your hands on."

Psalm 1 also shows that God wants you to prosper in all that you do. The whole point of this psalm is to encourage you to delight in the Word of God and to obey Him. God is telling you what you need to do in order to prosper in all that you do. Even when Joseph was thrown in jail, He continued to obey God—and God continued to make everything he touched prosper. In fact, that was Joseph's testimony throughout his life. From the minute he entered Potiphar's house until the day he died as second in command over Egypt, everything he put his hand to prospered. That can be your testimony too. When you obey God, you'll experience God's intervention again and again. His will is that you prosper in all that you do.

You Prosper in All that Pertains to You

When King David was moving the ark of the Lord back to Jerusalem, he stopped for three months and put the ark in the house of Obededom. Remember that the ark contained the presence of the Lord, so Obededom literally had God in his house. "The ark of the LORD continued in the house of Obededom the Gittite three months: and the LORD blessed Obededom and all his household" (2 Sam. 6:11). In three months, Obededom prospered so much that people noticed it. But God didn't only bless Obededom. As He did with Joseph, blessing all of Potiphar's house, God blessed Obededom's entire household: his wife, children, servants, livestock, everything, and everyone. It wasn't long before King David heard that "the LORD hath blessed the house of Obededom and all that pertaineth unto him, because of the ark of God" (v. 12).

God does not want to bless only you; He only wants to start with you. He wants you to be the impact point. He wants to drop the prosperity bomb on you and watch everything you touch be blessed. If you are a born-again believer, you're in a better position than Obededom was. He had the presence of God in his house in the form of an ark, but God is literally dwelling in your spirit (see John 4:24). How much more can you prosper in all that pertains to you because God is living on the inside of you?

You Prosper Everywhere You Go

When Joshua was about to go into the Promised Land with an untrained army, God gave him a battle plan and a promise: "Only be thou strong and very courageous, that thou mayest observe to do according to all the law, which Moses my servant commanded thee: turn not from it to the right hand or to the left, that thou mayest prosper withersoever thou goest" (Josh. 1:7).

That, of course, is exactly what happened. The walls of Jericho fell before him. Joshua had the Prosperous Touch everywhere he went.

Isaac did too. He was already prosperous because he was the son of Abraham, a prosperous man, but he became "holy rich" when he himself obeyed God and the blessing of God fell on his life (see Genesis 26). He became so rich, in fact, that the king of the nation he went to for help in a time of famine told him to get out because Isaac was wealthier than the nation itself. Everywhere he went, he dug wells and found water. Today we have a limited understanding of the context of this story and of how very precious water is in a time of famine, but for Isaac and his family, finding a well was akin to survival itself. Isaac increased everywhere he went because the blessing of the Lord was on his life—because he had the Prosperous Touch.

God's battle plan for Joshua and for Isaac is the same for you: do everything according to the Word, and everywhere you go, you will prosper. Even in places where it looks like you can't prosper, you will. You can even be in places where doors are closed to you or where the enemy has set a stronghold for you. When I fly, I'm never concerned about getting on an airplane, because when I do, it will be hijacked by angels instead of terrorists!

To prosper wherever you go, you must be led of the Holy Ghost. To ignore the leading of the Holy Ghost is to disobey God. "He will guide you into all truth: for he shall not speak of himself; but whatsoever he shall hear, that shall he speak: and he will shew you things to come" (John 16:13). He will guide you into all truth.

You Prosper All the Days that You Know

"If they obey and serve him, they shall spend their days in prosperity, and their years in pleasures" (Job 36:11). The implication here is that all their days, not some of their days, will be spent in prosperity, not in lack, not in vain. Every day will be a prosperous day. God's will is that you spend all your days in prosperity, not trying to get prosperity!

Not only that, but God promises you will spend your years—again, *all* your years, not some of them—in pleasures. When every day is a prosperous day, you'll be able to look back at the end of the year and say, "Bless God, this was a year full of pleasure!" That is the will of God for you.

Psalm 23 promises, "Surely goodness and mercy shall follow me all the days of my life: and I will dwell in the house of the LORD for ever" (v. 6). Psalm 91:16 says, "With long life will I satisfy him, and shew him my salvation." Living a long life is a promise of God throughout the Word. But why would it be a good thing if the life He called us to live was a sick, impoverished, and defeated life? Too many believers live as if Scripture says, "You serve Me, and you'll get by while you're fighting sickness, disease, depression, and poverty, and then you'll go to heaven where there are streets of gold." No! God has promised you the Prosperous Touch, whereby you spend your days in prosperity and your years in pleasure.

Thank God for giving you the prosperous touch in all that you do and in everything that pertains to you, everywhere you go and for all the days of your life!

GOD'S FUTURE FOR ME

1. What did you learn in this section that challenged you?

   _____

   _____

   _____

   _____

2. How has your thinking changed from "get it to get it" to "get it to give it" through this section?

   _____

   _____

   _____

   _____

3. At the end of the last section, you updated your understanding of what God's future for you is. Has it changed? Write your latest understanding of it.

   _____

   _____

   _____

   _____

4. Quote two Scriptures, one from the Old Testament and one from the New Testament, that show how God wants to bless you.

   _____

   _____

   _____

   _____

5. What are some of the areas besides finances that the Bible says God wants to bless you?

   _____

   _____

   _____

6. List the verses that God has quickened to you during this section. Use them as declarations during the next week to remind yourself of God's promises to you about your future.

_____

_____

_____

_____

Make Your Mark

Then this Daniel was preferred above the presidents and princes,
because an excellent spirit was in him; and the king thought to set him
over the whole realm.

— Daniel 6:3

— DAY 16 —

The Family Business

For this cause I bow my knees unto the Father of our Lord Jesus Christ, of whom the whole family in heaven and earth is named.

— Ephesians 3:14–15

In the first three sections of this book, we focused primarily on you and your future. Now it's time to take that to the next level—which is what this book is really about. Every person on this planet wants to live a fulfilled life where everything is great not just externally but in their hearts as well—yet that kind of life doesn't come just from receiving things. The life that God intends for you to have is not only one where you receive but one where you also give. I want you to have the future God wants you to have, but I also want you to help others do the same.

Recently, I watched a movie about an American pilot in World War II who volunteered to fight against the Nazis. One of his officers asked him if everyone from the United States was as eager to die as he was. "I'm not eager to die," the pilot responded, "but to matter."

Think about the day when you leave this earth. Do you want the planet to be better than it was when you got here? Do you want to leave your mark and make a difference? That is part of God's future for you, and in the coming days we're going to learn why He wants you to leave a mark and how you can do it.

In the Scripture verse for today, Paul says there is a family in heaven and on earth that is named after the Father God. That means more than the Butlers or the Jacksons or any other name you could come up with. It means every person who has received Jesus Christ as Lord of their life. We are all part of the same family, and we're all part of the family business, which is making sure that as many people as possible become a part of God's family:

Let your conversation be as it becometh the gospel of Christ: that whether I come and see you, or else be absent, I may hear of your affairs, that ye stand fast in one spirit, with one mind striving together for the faith of the gospel.

— *Philippians 1:27*

The family business is all about saving the world: "[He] will have all men to be saved, and to come unto the knowledge of the truth" (1 Tim. 2:4). Frankly, if it weren't for the fact that God uses us to save the world by reaching those who need to receive Him, we would already be in heaven because we already have our tickets punched. Because there

There comes a time when God expects you to go from being a consumer to being a contributor.

are so many who have yet to receive Him and become a member of the family of God, He has left us here and commissioned us all as a big family in the earth to do our part in helping Him save the world.

It is time for you to take your place in the family business if you have not already done so. That is when you will find yourself being fulfilled and living a life that matters. Sadly, too many Christians have not responded to this commission. "For when for the time ye ought to be teachers, ye have need that one should teach you again which be the first principles of the oracles of God; and are become such as have need of milk, and not of strong meat" (Heb. 5:12). There comes a time when God expects you to go from being a consumer to being a contributor, from being a receiver to being a giver, from being someone ministered to and being the one who ministers to someone else. God expects that you grow to a place where He uses you to be a blessing to someone else. God wants you to grow and then go.

Instead, we have the problem in the body of Christ of "fat sheep"—believers who come and get the Word week after week, year after year. The longer they sit in church without doing something, the harder it is to move them because they're too "overweight." If all you do is receive, you'll keep getting bigger and bigger and never give out and produce. If you can't figure out why your life isn't what it's supposed to be, maybe you have been receiving too long and need to start giving out. There's nothing wrong with receiving, but there's more to the Christian life than that. If all you did was inhale, then you would have a problem. You would turn blue and eventually not be here. You have to inhale and exhale.

And His gifts were [varied; He Himself appointed and gave men to us] some to be apostles (special messengers), some prophets (inspired preachers and expounders), some evangelists (preachers of the Gospel, traveling missionaries), some pastors (shepherds of His flock) and teachers. His intention was the perfecting and the full equipping of the saints (His consecrated people), [that they should do] the work of ministering toward building up Christ's body (the church).
— Ephesians 4:11–12, AMP

One reason we have church is not just to receive, but also to be equipped to do the work of the ministry. What good is it for a coach to spend all his time taking the team through training camp if they don't show up when it's time to play? What good is it if a drill sergeant trains his soldiers but they never show up on the battlefield? Jesus said, "Every branch in me that beareth not fruit He taketh away: and every branch that beareth fruit, he purgeth it, that it may bring forth more fruit...Herein is my Father glorified, that ye bear much fruit; so shall ye be my disciples" (John 15:2, 8). It looks like bearing fruit is important to God. He is saying you can be a believer but not a disciple; you're not a disciple until you are producing fruit—and fruit that remains (see v. 16). There are many other Scriptures that emphasize this, which I encourage you to read on your own (see Matthew 20:20–28; Mark 8:34–37; Luke 10:25–37; Romans 12:1).

How Do You Work in the Family Business?

One of the best ways to begin is by volunteering to serve in your local church. Acts 6 shows just how strategic this is. Some church historians say that just a few years after Pentecost, the body of Christ had grown to 100,000 members. They not only survived persecution but actually thrived and grew, and the church expanded widely—yet look at the seemingly small incident that threatened to shut down this miraculous growth:

In those days, when the number of the disciples was multiplied, there arose a murmuring of the Grecians against the Hebrews, because their widows were neglected in the daily ministration. Then the twelve called the multitude of the disciples unto them, and said, It is not reason that we should leave the word of God, and serve tables. Wherefore, brethren, look ye out among you seven men of honest report, full of the Holy Ghost and wisdom, whom we may appoint over this business.

— Acts 6:1–3

The entire move of God and expansion of the early church came to a halt because of a food fight! The apostles called together the church and picked seven men full of the Holy Ghost and wisdom who were set over this business. The entire church agreed, which is another miracle right there. They laid hands on them, put them in position, let them do their thing, and the church multiplied greatly (see v. 7).

What fixed the problem and took the church to the next level was people stepping up and doing their part. Somebody realized that it was no longer going to be the job of those up front to do that task. The people stood up and took their place, and as a result many more people missed hell and went to heaven.

A hundred years from now, no one is going to care about the kind of car you drove, house you lived in, or fashions you wore. No one is going to think about your hobby or your career. What will last is what you do for others, which is really what you do for God. There's no greater cause on this planet than the cause of the family of God. God has graced you with certain talents and abilities. He's done this because He and His family need your help. Take your place in the family business by using your God-given abilities to assist your local church, and help the family save the world!

Discovering the Future in You

Before I formed thee in the belly I knew thee; and before thou
camest forth out of the womb I sanctified thee, and I ordained
thee a prophet unto the nations.

— Jeremiah 1:5

When I was in high school, I got a full scholarship to attend the
University of Michigan, which is not easy to get. A full scholarship is
wonderful because you know there won't be any school loans to repay.
It's not something you pass up. The Lord, however, had other plans
for me once I graduated from high school. "I want you to go to Bible
school," He told me. In my mind, I figured I could attend Michigan first
and then go to Bible school after I graduated. Bible school wasn't
going anywhere, but the full scholarship would disappear quickly.

After graduating from high school, I started praying about it,
specifically asking when I should go—and God told me, "Now!" He
actually expected me to leave that scholarship and the career path I
had planned and go to an unaccredited Bible school in Broken Arrow,
Oklahoma! I had a choice to make. I decided to enroll in Bible school—
and I'm glad I did. God had a future for me, and Bible school was part
of it.

I'm not the only one who has a story like that. Everyone comes to a
Genesis 12 moment in their life when God calls them to do something,
like He did with Abraham, that makes no sense any way you look at
it—but you know that's what He's calling you to do. It's what you do
with that decision that determines whether or not you walk in the future
that God has for you.

The book of Jeremiah begins as the prophet tells how God called him: "Then the word of the LORD came unto me, saying, Before I formed thee in the belly I knew thee; and before thou camest forth out of the womb I sanctified thee, and I ordained thee a prophet unto the nations" (Jer. 1:4–5). Notice that even before God formed Jeremiah, He knew him and ordained a purpose for him: to be a prophet to the nations. Let me repeat that: God called him and ordained him *before* He even formed him.

It's the same with you. You actually existed before your mother and father came together and conceived you. Whether that was just in the mind of God or you were actually in heaven waiting to come, God knew you then. That's one of the reasons abortion is wrong. That's not a political statement but a biblical statement. God Himself says that He sanctified this child before he was even born. The word *sanctified* means "separated." Ordained means "I gave you." In other words God gave Jeremiah as a gift to the world.

> God called him and ordained him before He even formed him. It's the same with you.

Throughout Scripture, God called people with a specific purpose and anointing, announcing it either before they were born or after. God told Samson's mother that her son would begin to deliver Israel out of the hands of the Philistines. An angel announced to Mary that she would have a Son who would be the Savior of the world. The angel said the same words to Joseph: "He shall save his people from their sins" (Matt. 1:21). Jesus later confirmed that purpose by saying, "For this reason was I born" (see John 18:37). God called Abraham to be the father of many nations. David knew his assignment even as a teenager that he would become king of Israel, and through him would rise the King of kings. Paul knew his assignment would be to witness to the Jews, to the Gentiles, and even to stand before kings.

Each of these individuals in their own way was God's gift to the world. You, too, are God's gift to the world because He knew you before He formed you. You've been sent here for a purpose, even if you have yet to discover that purpose. Your purpose is as unique as you are. Consider that when you are driving on a highway, there are different kinds of vehicles around you. There are small cars, motorcycles, sedans, SUVs, and trucks of all sizes. They all are different and designed for a specific task. You don't take an SUV and try to haul cargo across the country. You could do it, but it would be very inefficient because that's not what an SUV is designed for.

It's the same with people. You've been designed for a specific purpose, but if you're not set in that purpose, it's no wonder you're not happy. No wonder it's hard for you to wake up every day and start all over again. You have the potential to be great at something, but if you don't know what it is, you're just getting through life. If you don't know God's purpose for you, it's time to get before Him to discover it. "If any of you lack wisdom, let him ask of God, that giveth to all men liberally, and upbraideth not; and it shall be given him" (Jas. 1:5). God doesn't want to keep His will a secret from you. If He's got a plan for your life, why would He hide it from you? He wants to make sure you know it so that you can fulfill it. So He says that if you lack wisdom and don't know what you're assigned to do, just ask Him. You can boldly go into the throne to ask (see Hebrews 4:16).

Notice James says that God "giveth to all liberally." God is a giver, not a taker. He's like a quarterback who has the ball and is looking down the field for somebody he can deliver it to. He didn't hike that football in order to hold it but to deliver it. That's how God is. His eyes are going to and fro over the earth, looking for somebody who will get into position so that He can tell them what their assignment is so that they can be fulfilled and be both blessed and a blessing. James also says that God "upbraideth not." He doesn't hold back.

Once you've asked God for wisdom, you don't need to keep saying, "God, show me. Show me. Show me." Believe that He has answered you and then just stay sensitive to hear His response (see Mark 11:24). If you have a hard time hearing from God, you don't need to look at Him but at yourself and do what is necessary to be sensitive enough to His leading.

How does God speak to us? God will probably not show up as a burning bush to you, and angels won't be coming down from heaven or riding across the sky announcing, "You are called to be an attorney." That's not how God speaks to us. He speaks to us through our spirits because God Himself is a spirit and communicates spirit to spirit. That happens in a number of ways.

First is the inward witness. You might have peace inside you or you might have a check in your spirit—something that tells you this is not God's path for you, even if it doesn't make sense to your natural mind. The Bible says to follow peace and not the lack of it. Sometimes I'll pray about something that looks like a good idea, but I don't have any peace about it in my spirit, so I don't do it. That doesn't necessarily mean it is evil but rather just not what God has assigned for me to do.

Second, God often leads by the still, small voice on the inside of your heart. Other times it's through the voice of the Holy Ghost, which you don't hear with your ears but hear inside you. The voice of the Holy Ghost is a little stronger than that still, small voice. When God told me to go to Bible school saying, "Now!" I never forgot it because it was almost like someone was in the same room saying, "Now!"

Other times, God leads us through visions and dreams—just remember that any dream or vision God gives you will line up with the Bible. If you have a dream you believe is from God but are not sure or you don't understand what it means, don't look for someone to give you the interpretation. If God was able to get that dream to you in the first place, He can also get the person to you with the interpretation.

The Motivational Gifts

In Romans 12, Paul lists what are often called the motivational gifts. These are part of your calling and can help you find God's purpose for you. Which of these best describes you: perceiver, teacher, exhorter, giver, administrator, or compassionate? I encourage you to study these and see how God has wired you. It will help you on your path to discovering specifically what He's assigned you to do in the earth. To help with this study, I recommend *How to Discover Your Purpose in 10 Days: God's Path to a Full and Satisfied Life* by Dr. J. Victor Eagan and Catherine B. Eagan.

Saying No to God

For some people, the point is not, "I don't know what I'm here to do" but rather, "I won't do it." What happens if you say no to God? He does give you the option of doing that, of course. He has set before you life and death, blessing and cursing. Choose life, that you may live (see Deuteronomy 30:19).

Remember what happened to Jonah. He knew perfectly well what God was calling him to do, but he literally ran in the other direction. "Jonah rose up to flee unto Tarshish from the presence of the LORD" (Jonah 1:3). Isn't that crazy to think we can hide from God? It's like our second daughter when she played hide-and-seek when she was younger. She would giggle and run to hide in the corner with her head sticking up over the couch. I could see her and she could see me, but she thought she was hiding.

That is what it's like when you talk about running from God. Do you think He can't see you? Don't you think He knows exactly where you are? When you run from God's purpose for you, it affects not only your future but also those around you: "Then were the men [on the ship] exceedingly afraid, and said unto [Jonah]. Why hast thou done this?" (v. 10). It can affect your husband or wife, kids, loved ones, church, and those to whom you were called to minister to so that their lives would have been blessed. Jeremiah tried to run from his calling and told God he wasn't going to prophesy anymore, but here's what happened: "His word was in mine heart as a burning fire shut up in my bones, and I was weary with forbearing, and I could not stay" (Jer. 20:9).

You can say no to God and enjoy a mediocre life. You might even be okay for a while. But eventually the curse will bring about some negative results. Or you can say yes to God and step into an adventure that will be wonderful. You can be the guy sitting and watching others on a roller coaster or you can get onto it, knowing that when the ride is over, it'll be great. You can give all the "buts" you want to, but it comes down to yes or no. Abraham had five years of mercy, but at some point mercy runs out. I gave up a full scholarship to the University of Michigan because God called me to Bible school, and I don't regret it for a moment.

You have to know your purpose and then say "Yes, God" to it. Don't wait any longer. Find out this week what you're called to do. If you already know and perhaps have been saying no to it, this week say yes and begin a journey to the wonderful life God has for you. When it's all said and done, you'll look back and say, "God, what a ride!"

— DAY 18 —

Be the Best

Then this Daniel was preferred above the presidents and princes, because an excellent spirit was in him; and the king thought to set him over the whole realm.

— Daniel 6:3

I'm a longsuffering Detroit Lions fan. A number of years ago, however, I rooted for the Indianapolis Colts because their coach, Tony Dungy, was a born-again believer and a strong man of God, not to mention a great coach. Under his leadership, the Colts won the Super Bowl. Coach Dungy used that platform as an opportunity to give God all the glory for what had happened in his life. Then he wrote a best-selling autobiography and testified about what Jesus had done for him. Many people who read the book would never walk into a church, but they heard the Gospel preached by a man who was the best in his field.

A few years ago, I rooted for the University of Florida football team, the Gators, because of their quarterback, Tim Tebow. Tebow is also a strong believer, as well as a Heisman Trophy winner. Before every game he would write a different Scripture verse on his face. The day he put John 3:16 on his face, 92 million people Googled it to find out what it said. You know they were not Christians because any Christian can quote that verse by memory. So this man—the best in his field— ministered the Gospel to 92 million people. And he was only about twenty years old at the time!

I can think of another young man who made a huge impact on the world around him: Daniel. When he was taken to Babylon along with many other Jews, God placed him before a king who ruled a good portion of the world at the time. Daniel refused to obey the government's command not to pray to anyone but the king, and as a result he was thrown into the lion's den. But God performed a miracle and the lions didn't get their dinner that night. Even the king knew it was a miracle and wrote a letter to the entire empire—millions and millions of people—telling them to worship Daniel's God. This would be like the president of the United States going on CNN, Fox, BBC, NBC, MSNBC, and every network you can think of, opening the Bible, and preaching Jesus to the entire world for fifteen minutes. The most powerful man on the planet preached about God because of a man God put in a position of influence.

There are many more ways to reach people and make your mark on the world besides standing up in a pulpit to preach. Sure, God uses pastors, but we put God in a box by thinking the only calling that influences the world is that of pastor or even a traditional missionary. Whatever God called you do is every bit as important as what God called me to do or any other preacher of the Gospel. First Corinthians 12 teaches that every part of the body has a role to play.

No matter where God has called you, if you want to leave a mark on the world around you, here is the key: you can't be mediocre. God didn't create you to be mediocre. He created you to be excellent. There's not a mediocre cell in your DNA. Your DNA is one of a victor, an overcomer, and a conqueror, so live up to what you are. God wants you to rise up in the ranks and become a person of influence. If He's called you to be a teacher, be the best one in your school district. If you're a sanitation engineer, own the company. If you're a lawyer, be the best. If you're an athlete, be the best. Whatever it is, take what God has given you and maximize it so that you can leave a mark on the world around you and help build God's kingdom on earth. God has sent you into the earth and pre-packaged you with the calling, anointing, gifts, and talents you need to carry out a specific assignment that will help build His church.

When Jesus called Peter, He said, "I say also unto thee, That thou art Peter, and upon this rock I will build my church; and the gates of Hell shall not prevail against it" (Matt. 16:18). The enemy is working overtime to build his kingdom, which is everyone in the world who has yet to receive Jesus. That's why Jesus warned Peter that the gates of hell would come against His church—and it's the same warning you need to receive about your calling. Those gates are designed to keep people in. Your goal is to get them out. That's why there's a huge war going on—a war for souls. Can you see why the enemy works so hard to keep you from your calling? If you are successful in carrying out your marching orders, you'll become a person of influence whom God will use to free people from Satan's future for them. Let God use you to help people live the future He has for them!

The Seven Pillars

Proverbs 9:1 says, "Wisdom hath builded her house, she hath hewn out her seven pillars." If we look at society, it seems there are seven pillars that hold it up, which are called the seven mountains of culture: family, religion, government, arts and entertainment, education,

> If we look at society, it seems there are seven pillars that hold it up, which are called the seven mountains of culture.

business and finance, and media and technology. Throughout history, when these pillars of society go from godly to ungodly, the nation itself follows the same path. We have seen that happening in our own country just in the past few generations. These mountains used to belong to God in America, but the enemy was able to penetrate them and take them for his purposes. Your job as a believer is to retake control of those mountains for God. You can do that by responding to God's call on your life, finding out which mountain He has called you to, and then working to be in a position of authority to make a difference in that mountain.

Let's look at each one of these mountains. As you read about them, let the Holy Ghost speak to you about which area He is calling you to.

Family

God created the family as the fundamental building-block of society: one man and one woman were married and had kids. Every empire throughout history that deviated from God's design for the family eventually crumbled. I don't have to tell you about the assault on the family that has happened in this generation, and we are paying the price for it. Thankfully, at the same time, God has been raising up godly families. Maybe your family isn't what the family unit was supposed to be, but you can start right now to take back that mountain in your life and show the world what family is supposed to look like.

Religion

In Matthew 24:4, Jesus warned us that in the last days there would be those who would rise up to deceive many people. We can sum this up by calling it false religion. America is in danger of no longer being a Christian nation. We see false religions spreading with greater influence over everyday life than ever: Islam, Buddhism, New Age, humanism, the occult, and more. The good news is Matthew 24:14, which tells us how to take back this mountain: "This gospel of the kingdom shall be preached in all the world for a witness unto all nations."

Government

Proverbs 14:34 says righteousness exalts a nation. It's not the Democrats, the Republicans, the Tea Party movement, health care, or Medicare. It's righteousness. So that must mean that unrighteousness makes a nation fail. The laws of our land were founded on righteous principles. This nation wasn't perfect by any means, but it was the most righteous in the world. However, that's changing as our governmental leaders are clearly guiding us away from God—and we have let them. How do we bring it back? Proverbs 29:2 says, "When the righteous are in authority, the people rejoice: but when the wicked beareth rule, the people mourn." So we take back the mountain of government by sending righteous, born-again, God-fearing Christians into politics.

Arts and Entertainment

This is another mountain that has dramatically shifted in the past generation and helped turn this nation from God. It's time to take back this mountain from the Satanic-inspired filth that it is spewing out in music, films, television, books, art, and more. If God has called you to take back this mountain from the enemy, don't let anybody tell you that you can't do it. Be the best you can be, and you will make a mark for the kingdom.

Education

The education mountain helps mold the next generation, so you know the enemy has been working diligently here. We need Christian teachers in public schools, and we need you to be the best. In fact, be the principal. Get on the school board. Take over the unions. Write the textbooks.

Business and Finance

We've seen this mountain crumble in the past few years, and we're all experiencing the fallout from it. God has called some people to make millions and millions of dollars. He may be calling you not just to work for a Fortune 500 company but to run that company. Don't let the world take those millions of dollars and dump it into things we don't believe in. Bring righteousness to this mountain. Take it back so that the righteous control the money and sow it into the kingdom of God.

Media and Technology

Some statistics say that 90 percent of people who work in the media are unchurched and even anti-God, which is why their perspective is what it is. God, however, has been raising up men and women in this mountain to take it back. If God has called you to journalism, be the best at it so that you can give people the truth.

Which of these mountains is God calling you to? Whichever one it is, be the best in it!

— DAY 19 —

Give God Your Best

This Daniel was preferred above the presidents and princes, because an excellent spirit was in him; and the king thought to set him over the whole realm.

— Daniel 6:3

We are learning how to make our mark in the world. Yesterday we studied the war that is raging around us between the kingdom of God and the kingdom of darkness, and we learned about the seven mountains where this battle is fought. We know the body of Christ is to take back each one of those arenas, and today we're going to learn more specifically how to do that.

I want to remind you about the blessings God promises to those who obey the covenant: "The LORD shall command the blessing upon thee in thy storehouses, and in all that thou settest thine hand unto; and he shall bless thee in the land which the LORD thy God giveth thee" (Deut. 28:8). He's not talking about a house or a car or a five-dollar bill. He's talking about what will get you those things—the root that will

The blessing is God's endowed power for prosperity and success.

produce that fruit. The house and car are the apples, but the blessing is the apple tree. The blessing is God's endowed power for prosperity and success. The word *endowed* means "clothing." In essence, God has given you a jacket. Whenever you put it on, it causes you to have supernatural success—not just earthly success but heavenly success. It's the kind of success where people look at you and say, "There's got to be something to this God thing because that's not normal."

This verse says that the Lord will command that kind of blessing on your storehouses and on everything you put your hand to. Whatever you touch prospers. Whatever project they give you at work, you put your hand to it and it prospers. That's the blessing God has promised you because you are in covenant with Him. It's the kind of blessing Joseph operated under when he went from being a slave in Potiphar's household to a position of authority. Why? Because his master saw that everything he touched prospered. I can just see Potiphar saying, "I'm going to get the most difficult task I can and give it to this young man and see if this is real." And it was.

You will be the best because you are blessed. The blessing will increase you, promote you, and put you in a place of influence where you can take back your mountain for the kingdom of God. You may say, "But I've been a born-again believer for thirty years; why haven't I experienced this kind of blessing?" It's as if someone gave you a brand-new Bentley and handed you the keys. You go out in your driveway and there it is. You put the key in and turn it, but the car never leaves your driveway. You can't imagine what you're doing wrong—it's not moving.

This is what is happening in the body of Christ today. We as believers are sitting in the Bentley. We've got the blessing of the Lord, but because we won't put our foot on the gas pedal, nothing is happening. You can have the blessing, but you still have to put it to work. You've got to do what it takes to be the best.

Does that sounds like you? I'm going to give you seven keys you can use to get that blessing moving in your life.

1. Be diligent. Many times, as Christians, we get great ideas and big dreams but don't want to get our hands dirty. We think, "It's just supposed to happen because I'm going to show up and the blessing will work. After all, 'I can do all things through Christ which strengthens me.'" It doesn't work that way. Proverbs 10:4 says, "He becometh poor that dealeth with a slack hand: but the hand of the diligent maketh rich." To be diligent means to consistently give 100 percent— that is, to consistently do your best. Notice that you can become poor or you can let God make you rich. You've got to do the work and do it with diligence.

2. Persevere. "A just man falleth seven times, and riseth up again" (Prov. 24:16). There are times when your intention is right but you blow it. And there are times when you are trying to be diligent and try something new but it fails. God doesn't give up on you. He has a "take two" for you—a second chance. You have to persevere. You have to keep going. You cannot quit. There should be no quitters in the body of Christ. God didn't quit on you, so you shouldn't quit on Him.

3. Aim for excellence. Why did the king keep promoting Daniel? It was because of his spirit of excellence: "This Daniel was preferred above the presidents and princes, because an excellent spirit was in him; and the king thought to set him over the whole realm" (Dan. 6:3). This guy aimed for excellence, and he hit the mark. If you do that, God will cause you to be preferred above many around you.

4. Do your research. "It is the glory of God to conceal a thing: but the honour of kings is to search out a matter" (Prov. 25:2). Even if you are already at the top of your field and have already had great success, there is still more you need to learn. "A wise man will hear, and will increase learning" (Prov. 1:5).

5. Find a mentor. Somebody has been where you're trying to go. Somebody has done what you're trying to do. Somebody has already overcome the obstacles you're facing right now. If you humble yourself and become teachable, they can help you not only do what they did, but do it better and faster. Or you can try to do it by yourself. God constantly used mentors. Isaac had Abraham. Jacob had Isaac. Elisha had Elijah. Timothy had Paul. The apostles had Jesus.

6. Walk in integrity. You can get to the place where you are the best but lose your influence. We see that happening right now in the world when people work their way to the top with great influence, but because of their lack of integrity they fall so low that they become the laughingstock of the world. As you develop your talent and gifting, make sure you develop your character at the same time so that you walk in integrity. "For bodily exercise profiteth little: but godliness is profitable unto all things" (1 Tim. 4:8). If you're watching bootleg cable, if your DVD player has a movie in it that just came out last Friday, if your iPod has music that you never purchased, if you're making money and not declaring it to the IRS, that is not walking with integrity. Do things God's way, and the blessing will work for you.

7. Give God the glory. "If any man speak, let him speak as the oracles of God; if any man minister, let him do it as of the ability which God giveth: that God in all things may be glorified through Jesus Christ" (1 Pet. 4:11). Our goal in life is to make Jesus famous. Do this in whatever sphere of influence God calls you to.

Give God your very best.

Faith It 'Til You Make It

Servants, be subject to your masters with all fear; not only to the good and gentle, but also to the froward. For this is thankworthy, if a man for conscience toward God endure grief, suffering wrongfully. For what glory is it, if, when ye be buffeted for your faults, ye shall take it patiently? but if, when ye do well and suffer for it, ye take it patiently, this is acceptable with God. For even hereunto were ye called: because Christ also suffered for us, leaving us an example, that ye should follow his steps.

— 1 Peter 2:18–21

What we're going to learn today has a major impact on helping you reach the position of success and influence God wants you have: how to properly handle a hater—someone who is in authority over you and consistently opposes you. You will undoubtedly encounter this no matter which mountain God calls you to work in, because remember that we are in a spiritual war. So you will face opposition. I'm going to focus on the workplace, but what I will share with you today applies to any one of the mountains God may call you to—any situation where there is an authority figure. If you learn it from the workplace perspective, you'll get it for everything else. Remember, you are about the family business, and that is to help people come to Jesus and have the future God wants them to have.

Let's start with the verses from 1 Peter 2. The word *servants* doesn't necessarily mean slave. Today we could say employee: "Employee, be subject to your employer, supervisor, manager, or boss." This entire passage is about those two words, "be subject." They mean "to yield."

They also mean another word we aren't too thrilled about: *submission*. When I start preaching about submission, I see people's body language change. Submission means to "yield to people, precepts, and principles that have been placed in your life as authorities." Throughout your life, someone is always in authority. At home it's your parents. In school it's the teacher or principal. In business it's your employer. At church it's your pastor. You can't just do whatever you want to do. At some point, you have to learn the principle of yielding to authority.

Peter not only says be subject to those in authority, but do it with fear. That word means "with reverence and respect." Do it with reverence and understanding that God is the one watching you. He sees your heart. Now, if that isn't hard enough, Peter says this applies not only to the "good and gentle" employers but to the "froward" ones, too. When I looked at the word *froward,* I knew it wasn't good. And when I looked up the meaning, I really knew it wasn't good. It means to be "warped and perverse, ill-tempered, harsh, overbearing, unreasonable." Who wants to yield to a boss like that? So I'm supposed to not only do what this knucklehead says, but I'm supposed to respect him with my heart?

Exactly.

How on earth can you do that? Here's how:

Servants, be obedient to them that are your masters according to the flesh, with fear and trembling, in singleness of your heart, as unto Christ. Not with eyeservice, as menpleasers; but as the servants of Christ, doing the will of God from the heart; with good will doing service, as to the Lord, and not to men: knowing that whatsoever good

Treat your boss like you would treat Jesus.

thing any man doeth, the same shall he receive of the Lord, whether he be bond or free.

— Ephesians 6:5–8, emphasis added

In other words, treat your boss like you would treat Jesus. Paul didn't say they were Jesus or even acting like Jesus. He said, "Work for them like you're working for Jesus"—because really, you are.

If we go back to the verses from 1 Peter, we see why God wants us to do this: "This is acceptable with God" (1 Pet. 2:20). One translation says it wins God's approval. Isn't that what you're looking for? If you're going to become the best, you need God's anointing and power.

God does not bless mess. You can't expect Him to promote you when you're telling off your boss. Even when your boss or any authority figure is a hater, God does not expect you to return evil for evil, try to get them back with revenge, or manipulate the situation so that they could get fired. Dog-eat-dog or survival-of-the-fittest is how the world gets ahead, but that's not how things work in God's kingdom. If you want to get ahead God's way, you have to do the complete opposite of what the world says.

You may be ready to throw away this book right now, but don't. You've gone through twenty days. Stay with me. If you need a little more convincing, look at Jesus. He didn't do anything wrong, either, but He allowed His enemies to beat Him and put Him on a cross without ever uttering a word.

Let's say your boss is coming down on you for something you didn't even do. It's not fair. You didn't do it. It's not your fault, but he's causing you to pay the price for it. You've explained—with respect—your side of the story, but he's not buying it. Because of your honor before God, you don't tell him off. You don't knock him out. You don't try to manipulate. You don't play office politics. You don't turn around behind his back and email everyone about it. When you do that, you've lost all chance of winning your boss to Jesus—and anybody else in your workplace who's watching you. You are no longer a light to the world. You are no longer salt to the earth. You have lost your savor and Satan has won.

So instead, this is how you react—because you are about the family business, and that is to help people come to Jesus and have the future God wants them to have. You say to yourself, "God is watching me, and I know He's the One who needs to handle this. I have faith that He's going to take care of it." And that's what I want you to see today. Sometimes you've got to faith it 'til you make it. I didn't say "fake it" but "faith it." You put your trust in God to handle your boss. That's faith. Faith is the belief that God will do what He said. Faith is not based on what you can see. Faith doesn't say, "I believe it because I see it." It says, "I believe it in spite of what I see." So your situation may look like the complete opposite of what you're believing for, and in fact it may look like it's getting worse, but because you believe God's Word, you choose to do what's right. You say, "I put my faith in God because I know He is going to work it out."

Here are three ways to help you handle a hater.

1. Communicate in love. You have a right to communicate even to somebody who is in authority over you, but you must do it in love. You don't repay hate with hate. "Speaking the truth in love…let no corrupt communication proceed out of your mouth, but that which is good to the use of edifying, that it may minister grace unto the hearers" (Eph. 4:15, 29). Your words must build up.

2. Pray fervently. "Pray one for another….The effectual fervent prayer of a righteous man availeth much" (Jas. 5:16). This type of prayer where you continue to seek God's face about a matter is called supplication. As you pray fervently, more of His power is pumped into your situation. Revelation 8:4 says your prayers are on an altar before God right now, coming up into His nostrils.

3. Overcome evil by doing good. "If thine enemy hunger, feed him; if he thirst, give him drink: for in so doing thou shalt heap coals of fire on his head. Be not overcome of evil, but overcome evil with good" (Romans 12:20–21).

I want to encourage you today that whatever hater is in your life, handle him or her according to God's way. Faith it 'til you make it. You will get your promotion. You will get your victory. And most importantly, you will help that person come to Jesus and have the future God wants them to have.

Toil No More

Christ hath redeemed us from the curse of the law.
— Galatians 3:13

If you're like most people, whether you have a full-time job outside your home or work full-time in your home, you spend between 60 and 70 percent of your life working. That's a very high percentage of your life. It means you spend more time working than you do relaxing with your family, enjoying a hobby, going to church, or enjoying any other area of your life. Who doesn't want a work life that is meaningful, has purpose, accomplishes something, and brings fulfillment? Nobody wants to spend 60 percent of their life miserable. Add to that the pressure of working to make a living, pay the rent, feed your children, and afford things to make your life enjoyable and you see why so many people—including believers—think a nine-to-five job or any kind of work is part of the curse.

Let's look back in Genesis to see what really happened.

In Genesis 1, this is Adam's reality: God put him in a garden that He had already created. There were fruit trees for him to eat—provision for him. He didn't have to toil to grow the fruit. Then God gave him an assignment and said, "You dress and you keep this garden. By the way, while you're carrying out your assignment you can eat from any of the trees of the garden except the tree of the knowledge of good and evil" (Gen. 2:15–17, paraphrased). I want you to notice that Adam's provision was not necessarily tied to his work. That fruit was already there. Dressing and keeping the garden would help God maintain the garden, but Adam didn't have to work so that he could eat. He worked because he had an assignment from God.

When Adam disobeyed God and ate from the only tree God told him not to eat from, a curse came upon his life: "Cursed is the ground for thy sake; in sorrow shalt thou eat of it all the days of thy life; thorns also and thistles shall it bring forth to thee; and thou shalt eat the herb of the field; in the sweat of thy face shalt thou eat bread" (Gen 3:17–19).

The word *sorrow* in Hebrew means "painful toil, grievous labor." So if the curse meant that work was sorrowful, then clearly before sin came in Adam's life, his work must have been enjoyable. Before the curse there was no sweat; after the curse there was sweat. Before the curse there was no toil; after the curse there was toil. Before the curse there was enjoyment; after the curse there was sorrow.

Too many Christians think that curse continues to this day, and as a result they toil in their jobs and think their work is what brings their provision. But I have good news for you. Adam caused the curse to be on man, and man lived under that curse for a long time, but the Bible says, "Christ hath redeemed us from the curse of the law" (Gal. 3:13). Oh, I am glad to be part of the "us"! And you are part of the "us," too. Jesus has set you free from the curse. How? He became a curse for you: "For it is written, Cursed is every one that hangeth on a tree: that the blessing of Abraham might come on the Gentiles" (vv. 13–14). I was not born a Jew; I was born a Gentile. And I am glad that now that I have received Jesus, I am grafted in to that blessing according to Romans 12:17–18. Now I can live under the blessing, and while I carry out my God-given assignment, the blessing empowers me to prosper and succeed, not just financially but in every area of my life. If you are a born-again believer in Christ, you are freed from that curse also.

"The blessing of the LORD, it maketh rich, and he addeth no sorrow with it" (Prov. 10:22). We have already seen that the blessing of the Lord is God's power to prosper and have success. So when God puts this blessing on your life, He does not add any sorrow to it. He does not give you the responsibility of toiling or sorrowing in your work to get that provision. The curse is an empowerment to fail, but the blessing of the Lord is an empowerment to prosper and have success.

So instead of your work being painful toil and grievous labor, instead of producing through the sweat of your face, now you have the blessing. You can go back to what Adam had in the beginning before the fall. Your work can be meaningful, enjoyable, and successful, and you can do it "sweatlessly." You can focus on completing your God-given assignment versus trying to make a living. Your toiling days are over.

You may have to make a major shift in your thinking and your actions as you realize what this means, but you won't be alone. Let's look at a few of Jesus's disciples and see how they had to shift their thinking

> Your work can be meaningful,
> enjoyable, and successful, and
> you can do it "sweatlessly."

from toiling to blessing. Peter was a fisherman, and one morning he was talking to Jesus after a long night of fishing with absolutely no catch. He and the other fishermen were on the night shift and hadn't caught a thing. That sounds like the curse to me.

Jesus said, "Launch out to the deep, and let down your nets" (Luke 5:4). Peter explained, "Master, we have toiled all the night, and have taken nothing" (v. 5). Jesus was talking about the kingdom and Peter was talking about toiling. Peter's thinking was that his provision was tied to his employment. For his entire life, his provision came through toiling, working hard, and the sweat of his face. He didn't understand that he was in the presence of the Blesser and that now the blessing was going to produce for him. He let out his net—and suddenly there were so many fish that the net broke. They called other fishermen to help load the fish into their boats, and there were so many fish that the boats started to sink.

Peter went from toiling all night and catching nothing to instantly receiving a net-breaking, ship-sinking harvest. As Kate McVeigh, author of *7 Habits of Uncommon Achievers,* says, "One day of favor is better than 1,000 days of labor." Your prosperity and your provision come from the kingdom. They come as a result of the blessing, not as a result of toiling all night.

Jesus's other disciples also had to change their way of thinking. In John 6, Jesus has just finished speaking to thousands of people and asked His disciples, "How are we going to feed all these people?"

Philip replied, "Even if we work for a months, we couldn't get that much money. We can't get that much money, Jesus. It's too late." Can you see how he was talking about toiling and that he tied provision to labor?

Andrew said, "There is somebody here with five loaves and two fishes, but what's that going to do?" We have to give Andrew a little credit; he starts off on the right track, but ends up on the wrong one.

You know what happened. Jesus took those five loaves and two fish, applied the blessing to them, and the blessing reproduced enough harvest to feed at least five thousand people—probably more like ten thousand or even twenty thousand (considering the women and children). There were even baskets full of food left over, and they didn't come from toiling, either; they were a result of the blessing.

Please recognize that you don't have to toil. Recognize that you work for a giving, not a living. Otherwise you are serving mammon, not God: "No man can serve two masters: for either he will hate the one, and love the other; or else he will hold to the one and despise the other. Ye cannot serve God and mammon" (Matt. 6:24). The word *mammon* means "wealth personified." The concept of toiling is really a symptom of serving mammon; you think you have to toil so that you can eat. You may be calling on the name of the Lord, but because you are still toiling and expecting provision that way, you are serving mammon.

I am not saying that God doesn't want you to work. I am not saying that God won't use your job to get money to you. I'm saying your provision is not necessarily tied to your employment, your education level, your seniority, or the economy. You live in an entirely different system where the blessing of the Lord is available to you—and that blessing can make you rich, and there will be no sorrow in it at all.

If it is time for you to switch systems and switch masters, please don't delay. Stop serving mammon with your actions while you are serving God with your mouth. From now on, serve God with your mouth and serve God with your actions. Instead of thinking you need a job to pay for your food, focus on your God-given assignment and God's blessing will provide for you abundantly. As you focus on your God-given assignment, you will make your mark for God and toil no more!

GOD'S FUTURE FOR ME

1. What did you learn in this section that forced you to change the way you think?

   _____

   _____

   _____

   _____

2. What does it mean to you personally to be part of the "family business"?

   _____

   _____

   _____

   _____

3. At the end of the last section, you updated your understanding of what God's future for you is. Has it changed now that you know about the seven mountains? Write your latest understanding of it, incorporating at least one of the seven mountains.

   _____

   _____

   _____

   _____

4. Quote two Scriptures, one from the Old Testament and one from the New Testament, that show that God wants you to make a mark in the world and empowers you to do so.

   _____

   _____

   _____

   _____

5. What did God speak to you about "toiling no more"?

   _____

   _____

_____

_____

6. List the verses that God has quickened to you during this section. Use them as declarations during the next week to remind yourself of God's promises to you about your future.

_____

_____

_____

_____

Save Your World

Howbeit Jesus suffered him not, but saith unto him, Go home to thy friends,
and tell them how great things the Lord hath done for thee,
and hath had compassion on thee.

— Mark 5:19

– DAY 22 –

Authentic

"Ye are the salt of the earth: but if the salt have lost his savour, wherewith shall it be salted? It is thenceforth good for nothing, but to be cast out, and to be trodden under foot of men."

— Matthew 5:13

I preached a sermon in which I held up two Gucci purses. They looked exactly the same, but one was an authentic Gucci and the other was a knock-off. Some Christians are a lot like that knock-off bag; they look like the real thing, but they're not authentic. They talk the talk but don't walk the walk. They say they're Christian, but when we actually look at their lives, they're not authentic.

In this final section of the book, we're going to study how God wants to use you to save the world. You can't be a knock-off believer and do that. He wants you to be an authentic believer. That's the only way you'll experience the future He has in mind for you and help people come to Jesus and have the future God wants them to have, too.

Let's study what an authentic believer looks like. In Matthew 5:13, Jesus said those who follow Him are the salt of the earth, but if that salt loses its flavor, it's good for nothing. In fact, He said you might as well get rid of it, throw it out, and let people walk all over it. He was talking to and about believers.

"Forasmuch as this people draw near me with their mouth, and with their lips do honour me, but have removed their heart far from me, and their fear toward me is taught by the precept of men" (Isa. 29:13). This passage refers to God's judgment coming upon a people who had removed their hearts far from Him. Notice God did not say far from church but "far from Me." You can be at church and be far from Him. You can serve and be far from Him. That's being a hypocrite—and we know what God has to say about that:

"Therefore when thou doest thine alms, do not sound a trumpet before thee, as the hypocrites do in the synagogues and in the streets, that they may have glory of men. Verily I say unto you, They have their reward....And when thou prayest, thou shalt not be as the hypocrites are: for they love to pray standing in the synagogues and in the corners of the streets, that they may be seen of men. Verily I say unto you, They have their reward....Moreover when ye fast, be not, as the hypocrites, of a sad countenance: for they disfigure their faces, that they may appear unto men to fast. Verily I say unto you, They have their reward."

— Matthew 6:2, 5, 16, emphasis added

Jesus uses the word *hypocrite* three times in these three verses—and there are many other places where He told people to their face, "You are a hypocrite." Obviously this meant something to Him. The

When you are not an authentic Christian, you're just playing a role, and it's not long before everyone knows it.

Greek word translated *hypocrite* means "an actor under an assumed character; stage-playing." When you are not an authentic Christian, you're just playing a role, and it's not long before everyone knows it. That's how parents can lose their kids. The children grow up watching their parents act like one thing in church, but the kids know they're really knock-offs based on how they live at home.

I have another word for knock-off Christians: practical atheists. They are people who believe that God exists but live life as though

He doesn't. They have no reverence for God. Someone can say, "I believe in God. I'm a Christian," but if you look at how they live their life, you wouldn't know it. Being a practical atheist leads you to being practically broke, practically sick and practically depressed. Here are three indicators of a practical atheist:[2]

You know it's wrong, yet you still do it. (See Proverb 8:13.)

You know it's right, but you refuse to do it. (See Luke 6:46.)

You know He needs you, yet you refuse to serve. (See Isaiah 6:8.)

If that describes you, it's time to stop playing Christian. It's time to be salt that has flavor, not the kind that has lost its flavor and is good for nothing but being trodden underfoot. You can't cheat on your wife or husband and think other people don't know about it. You can't diss your boss behind his back and think God doesn't see. You can't cheat on your income taxes and think He doesn't notice. It's time to be an authentic believer, not a knock-off. If you need to make a correction, make a correction.

What Authentic Believers Look Like

1. Authentic believers are obedient. "As obedient children, not fashioning yourselves according to the former lusts in your ignorance: but as he which hath called you is holy, so be ye holy in all manner of conversation; because it is written, Be ye holy; for I am holy" (1 Pet. 1:14–16). When you're an authentic believer, you're like an obedient child who does what he's told. You don't conform to your former lifestyle. Or, as the Message version of this passage says, you "don't lazily slip back into those old grooves of evil, doing just what you feel like doing. You didn't know any better then; you do now."

2. Authentic believers are holy. The one who called you is holy, and He's calling you to be holy, also, which here means "morally blameless, consecrated, and set apart." God is calling you to be holy in your lifestyle, holy in your marriage, holy in how you handle your business, holy in how you spend your money, holy in your words, holy in everything. He says, "I'm holy; be like Me" (see 1 Peter 1:16).

3. Authentic believers are set apart. There are certain words you're not going to use anymore, certain music you're not going to listen to, and certain ways you're going to handle your money and act on your job. People might look at you like you're crazy and talk about you, but you're just going to act different from the world. You are set apart.

4. Authentic believers are disciples. "Then said Jesus to those Jews which believed on him, If ye continue in my word, then are ye my disciples indeed" (John 8:31). Here, Jesus was speaking to believing Jews who recognized He was the Messiah. They were obviously already believers, but He was telling them what they needed to do to be His disciples: continue in His word. In other words, stay or dwell in the Word. The word *disciple* is used two ways in the Scripture. One of them is simply a follower of Jesus. The other is used in this verse from John. Here, a disciple is one who is like Him.

"Go then and make disciples of all the nations, baptizing them into the name of the Father and of the Son and of the Holy Spirit, teaching them to observe everything that I have commanded you, and behold, I am with you all the days (perpetually, uniformly, and on every occasion), to the [very] close and consummation of the age. Amen (so let it be)."

— Matthew 28:19–20, AMP

You have to tell people about Jesus and lead them to salvation, but that's not the end of it. They're not a disciple yet! They become a disciple when they observe or follow what Jesus taught. An authentic believer is a disciple and a disciple-maker.

5. Authentic believers love one another unconditionally. Jesus said, "A new commandment I give unto you, That ye love one another; as I have loved you, that ye also love one another. By this shall all men know that ye are my disciples, if ye have love one to another" (John 13:34–35).

6. Authentic believers produce much fruit and thereby glorify God. "Herein is my Father glorified, that ye bear much fruit; so shall ye be my disciples" (John 15:8).

Five Keys to Being Authentic

When you live the life that the Word of God says you're supposed to live—the life of an authentic believer—that's when God can use you and bless you according to His plan for your future. Authentic believers are the ones who walk in health, walk in wealth, and have wonderful marriages and life-changing testimonies. Here are five keys to help you be an authentic believer.

1. Deposit God's Word in your heart. "Thy word have I hid in mine heart, that I might not sin against thee" (Ps. 119:11).

2. Protect your heart. "Keep thy heart with all diligence; for out of it are the issues of life" (Prov. 4:23).

3. Do life together with other authentic believers. "He that walketh with wise men shall be wise" (Prov. 13:20).

4. Regularly attend church services and small group meetings. "Forsake not the assembling of yourselves together" (see Hebrews 10:25).

5. Develop a prayer life. "Watch and pray, that ye enter not into temptation: the spirit indeed is willing, but the flesh is weak" (Matt. 26:41).

— DAY 23 —
Not Ashamed

I am ready to preach the Gospel....For I am not ashamed of the gospel of Christ: for it is the power of God unto salvation to every one that believeth.

— Romans 1:15–16

Webster's 1828 Dictionary defines the word *shame* as a "painful sensation excited by a consciousness of guilt or of having done something which injures reputation, an embarrassment." The word that jumps out at me here is *reputation*. Paul told the Romans that he was not ashamed to preach the Gospel. Jesus warned, "Whosoever therefore shall be ashamed of me and of my words in this adulterous

The enemy tries so hard to keep us silent because he knows that the Gospel is the power—the POW—of God.

and sinful generation; of him also shall the Son of man be ashamed, when he cometh in the glory of his Father with the holy angels." (Mark 8:38). When Jesus comes back to the earth, I don't want Him to be ashamed of me.

The enemy tries so hard to keep us silent because he knows that the Gospel is the power—the POW—of God. When you speak God's words, people have access to the POW of God. God's power backs up what you say, and it produces salvation—not just someone being born again but getting healed, prospering, being protected, and living the life God intends for them.

We live in a world today, particularly in the United States, where there is a concerted effort to silence Christians, to make Christianity a private faith, and to persecute anyone who tries to keep it a public faith. I don't just mean politically, but for individuals. Too many believers are ashamed to show the world that they love and serve Jesus. They're ashamed to preach the Gospel to those around them who need it, even though they know what the Gospel will do for them. We don't need any secret-agent Christians right now, especially at a time when the world is coming out of the closet with every disgusting thing the enemy encourages them to do. As they come out of the closet, we as the church, who have the Gospel of Jesus, are getting into the closet because we're concerned about what someone may think of us. Yet God needs us to win the world around us. The only way we are going to do this is by glorifying God in our spirit, soul, body, and lifestyle twenty-four hours a day, seven days a week, and 365 days a year in every arena of life.

So here's the problem. You can't do what God needs you to do and what others need you to do if you are ashamed of Jesus and what you believe. You can't do it if you're afraid of what the world may think about you and how your reputation may be hindered. Today is decision day for you. You need to decide you will no longer be ashamed. You need to decide to come out of the closet and be bold.

Do we begin again to commend ourselves? Or need we, as some others, epistles of commendation to you, or letters of commendation from you? Ye are our epistle written in our hearts, known and read of all men: forasmuch as ye are manifestly declared to be the epistle of Christ ministered by us, written not with ink, but with the Spirit of the living God; not in tables of stone, but in fleshy tables of the heart.

— 2 Corinthians 3:1–3

You are a letter written by Jesus to a lost world. You are an open book that sinners and saints alike can look at and say, "That book was written by Jesus. She's all about Jesus. She's one of those Jesus folk."

If you've ever taken your kids to a zoo or a museum, you know there are signs in front of the exhibits that explain what you're seeing. Your child points at an animal and asks, "What's that?" and you say, "It's a bird." "What kind of bird?" Laid out for you is all the information you need about that bird so you can answer the eighty questions your seven-year-old is going to ask you. Paul is saying that you are like that sign for non-believers. They see you and you're like an open book in front of them showing them, "This is a Christian. This is somebody who loves God. This is somebody serving Jesus." At least, I hope that's what they see when they read you because you're what Jesus is using to talk to the world. You are His tool to get information and revelation to the world. You are His love letter to the world. Someone once said, "Of one hundred unsaved men, one will read the Bible and ninety-nine will read the Christian."

Paul says that the words to this book are not written with ink but with the Holy Ghost. People who read your book should see love, joy, peace, patience, longsuffering, goodness, and mercy. These words aren't written on tablets of stone or paper but on your heart. People can't see your heart with their natural eye, but they can see it by your actions. So the world looks at you and watches how you live as a Christian and the results of Him working in your heart. They can see how He's changed you. They can see how you operate in love, when maybe in the past you would have operated in hate. They can see how you respond to that boss everyone else hates, when in the past maybe you did too. They can see how you give, when in the past you may have hoarded.

This is God's plan for your life. This is what God wants you to live. This is part of being a Christian, but you can't be that way if you are ashamed of the Gospel. You can't live a private Christianity and at the same time let the world read the book He's written on your heart.

"For from you sounded out the word of the Lord not only in Macedonia and Achaia, but also in every place your faith to God-ward is spread abroad; so that we need not to speak any thing" (1 Thess. 1:8). The Message Bible says, "Your lives are echoing the Master's

Word." You are the echo of Him. You are the reverberation. Paul says, "The news of your faith in God is out. We don't even have to say anything anymore—you're the message!"

You can start out very bold and with good intentions, but persecution and a few backstabs from the world can quickly stop your best intentions. When Timothy faced that, Paul wrote to him, "Be not thou therefore ashamed of the testimony of our Lord" (2 Tim. 1:8). Paul stirred up the faith in Timothy. That is my goal today: to stir you up and get you back to the place where you will be bold once again, so that you will recognize you're not the lamb but the lion. Jesus never asked you to be the lamb. He was the lamb for you so that now you can be like Him, a lion in this world.

"Ye are the light of the world. A city that is set on an hill cannot be hid. Neither do men light a candle, and put it under a bushel, but on a candlestick; and it giveth light unto all that are in the house. Let your light so shine before men, that they may see your good works, and glorify your Father which is in heaven."

— Matthew 5:14–16

You are God's letter that the world is going to read to find out about Him. Make your decision today that you will no longer be ashamed of the Gospel. You will be bold in the Holy Ghost.

I Dare You

Then they said one to another, We do not well: this day is a
day of good tidings, and we hold our peace: if we tarry till the
morning light, some mischief will come upon us: now therefore
come, that we may go and tell the king's household.

— 2 Kings 7:9

When we were kids and someone would say, "I dare you to do it,"
you knew it was something risky. Today I'm going to challenge you
to act on what we learned yesterday. In fact, I double-dog dare you. I
dare you to open your mouth and start telling people about the Jesus
you serve. I dare you to start telling them they need to receive Him. I
dare you to try to make as many disciples for Jesus as you can before
you leave this planet. I dare you. I am issuing a challenge to you today
because an authentic believer tells people about Jesus.

In 2 Kings 7, an enemy army seized the city of Samaria, and the
people suffered a great famine. God gave His people victory using the
footsteps of four lepers. When the lepers came to the enemy's camp,

**I dare you to go and tell them about
Jesus and the wonderful future He has
for them.**

they found food, clothes, and treasures. They immediately began eating, and finally one of them said, "This isn't good. This is not right. Here we are eating and enjoying ourselves but everybody in our city is starving and suffering. Shouldn't we go back and share this with the others?" (v. 9, paraphrased). Someone once said, "Christianity is one beggar telling another beggar where he found bread."

Those of us who have received Jesus as Lord of our lives have found something, and it is wrong for us to come together and have a good time on Sundays, Wednesdays, and in small groups but ignore the dying world around us by not telling them the truth about Jesus. And I'm not talking about taking up an offering once a year to fund missionaries to fulfill the Great Commission for us. We need to do what is right. That's why I dare you to go and tell them about Jesus and the wonderful future He has for them. It's time to tell it.

As I'm working on this chapter, my football team, the Detroit Lions, is about to start a new season. We think this year is going to be different because we have a new running back. The guy is just electric. Now, what would happen if he decided not to get on the field for the next game because he realized someone was going to tackle him? The fans would say, "Uh, yeah, you're going to get tackled. In fact, you're going to get hit hard, but we expect you to get on the field anyway. Hopefully you'll get around them or go through them to end up in the end zone a couple of times and it'll all be worth it."

You cannot stop telling people about Jesus simply because you might get tackled a few times. You need to get out there on the field and tell people about Him because if you keep doing what God said, eventually you're going to find yourself in the end zone with a bunch of other people and you'll be praising and worshiping God. They'll be joining you because you obeyed Him.

I want to show you some examples from the New Testament of people who preached the Gospel in spite of great opposition. The first one is Jesus Himself. One day He was in the temple, picked up the scrolls, read Isaiah 61, and said, "This day is this scripture is fulfilled in your ears" (Luke 4:21). Here's what happened: "When they heard these things, [they] were filled with wrath, and rose up, and thrust him out of the city, and led him unto the brow of the hill whereon their city was built, that they might cast him down headlong. But he passing through the midst of them went his way" (vv. 28–30). Can you imagine this? What's amazing to me is that He knew this was going to happen and still chose to speak the truth about who He was in the hope that at least some of them would believe. That takes great boldness.

In the book of Acts, there are numerous examples of believers who dared to preach the Gospel in spite of life-threatening opposition. In chapter 3, God healed a lame man, and as a result four thousand people got saved. Peter was dragged before Annas and Caiaphas, the very people who sentenced Jesus to death, to explain what happened. How would you feel if you were dragged before these men? A little hesitant? They asked, "By what power, or by what name, have ye done this? Then Peter, filled with the Holy Ghost said unto them…by the name of Jesus Christ of Nazareth, whom ye crucified, whom God raised from the dead, even by him doth this man stand here before you whole….Neither is there salvation in any other: for there is none other under heaven given among men, whereby we must be saved" (Acts 4:7–10, 12). Peter dared to speak the truth to the very people who conspired to kill the Lord, knowing he could have been killed too.

In Acts 8, believers were persecuted and scattered abroad, running for their lives. How did they go? "Preaching the word" (v. 4). Wait a minute—isn't preaching the Word what got them in trouble in the first place? The whole point of running was so that people would not know that they were Christians, right? No. They did have to get out of that situation, but they understood their responsibility to tell people about Jesus. They understood they carried the greatest message in the history of mankind, so even though they were running for their lives, they were still preaching Jesus, knowing it could cost them everything they had. What the enemy meant for evil by attacking them, God turned around for good because those believers spread all over the region and thousands more came to know Him. We are here today partly because of them.

We move on to Acts 21, where we have a story that is worthy of a movie. Paul is preaching and a mob is ready to kill him. The Roman soldiers get in on the act and carry him away while the angry mob is still trying to kill him. In the midst of this scene, Paul says to the soldiers, "Let me talk with them." I don't know about you, but if a mob was trying to kill me, the first thing I'd say is, "Get me out of here!" Even though I love Jesus and want people to go to heaven, I'd want out of that situation as fast as possible. Not Paul. He got the crowd quieted down, "and when there was made a great silence, he spake unto them in the Hebrew tongue, saying, Men, brethren, and fathers, hear ye my defence which I make now unto you" (Acts 21:40–22:1). Paul dared to preach the Gospel, despite the fact that his life was in danger.

The history of the early church is one of persecution and expansion. It goes hand in hand. We are in a time today that the Bible calls the last days and, yes, persecution is rising against us. If you let people know you are a Christian, there is a very good chance they are going to have a problem with it, but God promised: "I've given you authority over all the power of the enemy and nothing by any means shall hurt you" (see Luke 10:19); "No weapon thrown against you shall prosper" (see Isaiah 54:17); "No evil shall befall you. A thousand may fall by your side, ten thousand by your right hand, but it will not come near you" (see Psalm 91:7); "You can do all things through Christ who strengthens you" (see Philippians 4:13). We can go on and on and on.

God has given you the power to carry His message to the ends of the earth—or around your block. God's power will back you up. God will use you to say the right words to people that will change their lives. He will use you to heal the sick, cast out devils, raise the dead, and do mighty exploits. You simply have to be bold enough to say, "I don't care what you say to me. I don't care how you threaten me. I don't care if you like me or if you don't like me. I am going to tell you the truth because I love you and I know God loves you, too."

Here are four keys to start "telling it":

- **Accept the responsibility to tell others in your life about Jesus.**

- **Establish a relationship with people (see Jesus's example in Matthew 9). Win by being a friend.**

- **Share your story. Paul used his testimony six times in the book of Acts.**

- **Give a personal invitation to receive Jesus. Pray the prayer of salvation with them (see Romans 10:9–10).**

Peter met Jesus because Andrew brought him. How many Peters are in your world right now? Your assignment this week is to find at least one person who could use a little more of that love and invite them to come with you to church or your small group or to receive Jesus on the spot.

I dare you to do it.

Every Success Is a Prayer Success

And in the morning, rising up a great while before day, [Jesus] went out, and departed into a solitary place, and there prayed.

— Mark 1:35

Jesus must have had an exhausting night with not much sleep. A few verses before this one quoted above, we find that Jesus was staying at Peter's house, where the entire city had come the night before to see Him. Imagine your entire city showing up on your doorstep asking for prayer! Jesus healed every sick person, cast out devils, and ministered to everyone who showed up. Notice that verse 35 does not say, "And in the morning Jesus slept in." It doesn't say he hit the snooze button and went back to sleep, over and over again. It says He got up in the morning before the day even began. That doesn't mean 7:00 a.m. or even 6:00 a.m., when it was probably daylight. He got up "a great while before day." He didn't just sit at the foot of His bed and talk to His Father. He got up, got dressed, found a solitary place, and prayed.

Why would Jesus, the Son of God, after a long night of ministry, still get up early to pray? A few verses later, we see that Simon and the others followed after Him. Jesus said to them, "Let us go into the next towns, that I may preach there also: for therefore came I forth" (v. 38). So Jesus had a long night of ministry, slept a few hours, immediately headed into a time of prayer, and then said, "It's time to go to the next town."

From that time of prayer, Jesus accessed the power of God. Prayer produced the power. It's the power that produces the success. If you look at Jesus's ministry throughout the Gospels, you see this pattern many times. In Matthew 14, Jesus spent all night on a mountain in prayer. The next thing that happened was He walked on water. So prayer preceded a great act of power. In Mark 9, the disciples tried to help a young man who was possessed with a demon spirit but didn't have any success, but when Jesus ministered to the young man, he was instantly freed. The disciples later asked why they couldn't cast out the demons, and Jesus replied, "This kind cannot be driven out by anything but prayer and fasting" (v. 29, AMP). If that is true, when did Jesus pray and fast? In the passage from Mark, He came down, saw

> The longer you spend in God's presence, the more His power gets rubbed on you.

the father, saw the boy, and cast out the demon spirit. He didn't say, "I'll be back after three days of prayer and fasting." He took care of it right then—because He had already prayed and fasted. He had already given birth to this boy's deliverance in His prayer time. That success was a prayer success.

If Jesus felt the need to spend time in prayer before ministry, you must need it, too. You absolutely cannot reach a sick and dying world without spending time alone with God in prayer. There's an exchange that happens when you earnestly seek Him for the lost. He gives you His wisdom and His power. The longer you spend in God's presence, the more His power gets rubbed on you. Every success is a prayer success first. That is one of our ten values at my church. We want to be successful in saving our families and others around us, and for that to happen, we must begin this process in prayer.

When you go on a job interview, you dress for success. You don't wear your ragged jeans and a dirty shirt. In the same way, when you go to minister to someone, you need to pray for success. You have to start the process in prayer, and as you pray for them and talk to God about their situation, God will give you wisdom. God's power will be rubbed on you, and when the time comes for you to tell them about Jesus, your words will have an impact in their hearts.

How Do You Pray "Successful" Prayers?

When Paul wrote to the church of Galatia, which had backslidden, he said, "My little children, of whom I travail in birth again until Christ be formed in you" (Gal. 4:19). The word *travail* means "to work." So it sounds like Paul was working something out. He used the phrase "travail in birth," which gives the mental picture of a woman in labor. In fact, a number of translations of this verse talk about birth pains and the birthing process. Paul is telling the Galatians that he is giving birth to something in their life.

We see this in other places throughout the Bible: "Epaphras… labor[ed] fervently for you in prayer" (Col. 4:12). "Strive together with me in your prayers" (Rom. 15:30). Paul was giving birth to them in prayer. This is clearly not the type of prayer where you just go before God and say: "Hey, Father God. I love Sam. He's my best friend. He's going to hell. Father, can You send somebody to help? Save him, Lord."

That's not travailing in prayer. Fervent, travailing prayer means you contend for your friend. You find out what the Bible says and pray that. You pray in other tongues for him. The Holy Ghost will help you to pray out the details of his life and his situation. This is an example of fervent prayer where you travail and contend for your friend:

"Father, thank You for Samuel. I ask that that You begin to deal with his heart about the truth about You. Cause the eyes of his heart to be enlightened and help him to see the truth. Send laborers across his path, me and others, to minister to him in a way in which he can receive it. I pray that You give me boldness to speak the Word of God, and indeed, cause miracles, signs, and wonders to be done as I minister to Samuel's life. Father, I pray these things in Jesus's name. Amen."

Then begin to pray in other tongues for the person, until you have a release in your heart that you've completed that prayer assignment that day.

That's just the short version. Travailing in prayer is something you don't accomplish in one minute or even one prayer session with God. It should be a regular part of your prayer life. James 5:16 says, "The effectual fervent prayer of a righteous man availeth much." Notice, this Scripture did not say, "The prayer of a righteous man availeth much." It uses the words *effectual* and *fervent*. We don't necessarily use those words in modern-day speaking, but the Amplified Bible gives us a good explanation of what they mean: "The earnest (heartfelt, continued) prayer of a righteous man makes tremendous power available." In other words, prayer is not about saying some words or even the right words. True prayer comes from the heart. If it is not coming from your heart, you are just being religious. Christianity is not a religion; it's a relationship. When you pray for other people, you need to pray from your heart, which means you ought to care about them and care about the situation they are in. Kenneth Hagin talked about identification in prayer—getting yourself to a place where you are identifying in your prayers with what the other person is going through. You put yourself in your friend's situation, almost making yourself feel his emotions, recognizing what his life must look like, and using that as fuel to help you to pray fervently for him.

There's another word in that Scripture that is vitally important to making sure your prayers for the lost are answered: *righteous*. "The effectual fervent prayer of a righteous man availeth much." You cannot live your life violating the Word of God and expect there to be any power in your prayers. You can look at the life of Samson to see that.

If there's sin in your own life, how are you going to pray for God to remove it from someone else's life? What you do in your private life makes a difference. If you are not living right, it is going to have an impact on whether you can win other people to Jesus. At the very least, why would that person want your Jesus if they see you doing the same thing they are doing? And even if they don't see it, it's affecting your prayers. That prayer power you need is not going to be there for you if you're not living a righteous life. Life is about choices. Every choice has a consequence. God is a God of mercy, so He will give you all kinds of time and send people your way, but at some point the laws of His kingdom will kick in.

Make a decision today to live a righteous life and to pray effectively and fervently for the lost world around you. Remember, every success is a prayer success first.

— DAY 26 —

Win by Being a Friend

"Go home to thy friends, and tell them how great things the Lord hath done for thee."

— Mark 5:19

In the passage above, we see one of the few times in Scripture where Jesus tells someone who wanted to follow him, "No, you can't." The man had been possessed with a legion of demon spirits, and when Jesus cast out the demons, the restored man wanted to go with Him. Jesus, however, told the man to go home to his friends and tell them what God had done for him. Imagine what a sacrifice it was for this man to leave the One who had finally healed him, but he did, and the Bible says many from his city received Jesus into their lives as a result.

What Jesus asked this man to do is what He wants all of us to do: go to those we care about—our family, friends, neighbors, and co-workers—and tell them what God has done for us. This is very different from confrontational soul winning, which is walking up to a stranger and saying, "Hey, you need Jesus. If you were to die today where would you end up?" There is a place for that, and some people do receive Jesus that way, but 80 percent of people who make a decision to follow Jesus do so as a result of a conversation with a family member or friend, not because some stranger walked up to them.

Who led you to the Lord? Strangers may have witnessed to you, but it was probably a friend or family member who really helped you receive Jesus. That's because you knew that person, trusted them, had a relationship with them, and saw Jesus in their life. Most of the time you

Who led you to the Lord? Strangers may have witnessed to you, but it was probably a friend or family member who really helped you receive Jesus.

are going to introduce people to Jesus simply by being a friend. I'm talking genuine friendship—not something you manipulate just to get them to meet Jesus.

I want to give you five keys to help you do this.

1. Discover the people who are God's focus for you. In Acts 16, God specifically gave Paul and Timothy their ministry focus: "[They] were forbidden of the Holy Ghost to preach the word in Asia" (v. 6). Later on, when they tried to go to Bithynia, "the Spirit suffered them not" (v. 7). Weren't there needs in Asia and Bithynia? Absolutely, but they weren't God's focus for Paul and Timothy at that moment. Instead, a man appeared to Paul in a vision and said, "Come over into Macedonia, and help us" (v. 9). You don't get to pick your city. You don't get to pick your person. The Lord had a city in mind and a focus for Paul and Timothy, and by the time God got finished, they gave birth to a great church called the Philippian church.

In Acts 8, the Holy Ghost led Philip to go into the desert and speak to an Ethiopian eunuch. He was God's focus and was hungry to learn more. Philip gave the man the truth, and the man went back to his country and led many to know Jesus.

Who is God's focus for you right now? If you already know, great. If you don't, do what we studied yesterday: fervently seek God in prayer.

2. Be a friend to them. I didn't say be a prophet or priest. I said to simply be a friend. You will be following the example of Jesus. In Matthew 9, Jesus called Matthew, a tax collector, to follow Him. Tax collectors were corrupt men who could burst into anyone's home and demand whatever they wanted, saying it was for back taxes. In the next verse, we see Jesus having dinner at Matthew's house, surrounded by all of Matthew's friends. Now, we can imagine what that was like. There was Jesus, Peter, John, and others dining with a fornicator, a liar, a cheater, an adulterer, a murder, and a tax collector.

The Pharisees and religious people went crazy and accused Jesus of being a sinner. Jesus didn't care. He was building a relationship with these people, and in Luke 15 we find out why. When Jesus started to preach, who came to hear Him? The publicans and sinners. Isn't that something? Since when do people who are stealing money eagerly come to church to hear the preacher? Yet they came to hear Jesus talk about how God leaves the ninety-nine to get the one. They listened because He was their friend.

One minister said, "Intelligent, caring conversation opens the door for evangelism of nonbelievers faster than anything else."[3] This is not talking about ambushing people or going after them for notches on your evangelism belt. This is you trying to save their life. Just talk to people. Get to know them. Find out what's going on in their lives. Show some true interest in them. Care about them like Jesus would. You've probably heard the statement, "People are not going to pay any attention to what you know until they know how much you care." So you truly have to be a genuine friend to them.

3. Meet a need. When Jesus spoke to the woman at the well, He started by meeting a need. She was thirsty, and He told her how she could never thirst again. "Hey, I can live with that," she said. "Give me that kind of water" (in John 4:15, paraphrased). When the conversation was over, she ran back to her town and told everyone what she'd heard.

When Jesus gave us the Great Commission, He wasn't talking about Christians laying hands on or healing only other Christians. He was talking about us laying hands on Christians and non-Christians. When you pray for non-Christians and they receive healing, later they will return to ask for an explanation. That opens the door for you to tell them about Jesus. I'm not talking about people getting healed inside the four walls of church but rather you going out and doing what Jesus said. Somebody talks to you about how their marriage is falling apart. They don't know what to do. You don't have to preach a whole series of messages to them, but you give them one good thing from the Word of God and tell them to go home and try it out. They come back and say, "Hey, that worked!" And that opens the door for you to continue to talk with them until you can introduce them to Jesus.

4. Be led. When you received Jesus into your life, the Holy Spirit came to live in your heart to help lead you and guide you. He does it many ways: by the Word, by the inward witness, by the inward voice, and by visions and dreams. Of course all of this depends on your having a prayer life. God knows the button that will help someone to see the truth. So don't limit Him with the Four Spiritual Laws or the Romans Road to Salvation. Thank God for those tools, but sometimes God will lead you to say something a little different than what you had planned. You need to flow with that.

5. Preach Jesus. That's simple, isn't it? When Philip was talking to the Ethiopian eunuch, he "opened his mouth...and preached unto him Jesus" (Acts 8:35). You can't do any better than preaching Jesus. The spirit of prophecy is the story of Jesus (see Revelation 19:10). When someone is in sin, you don't judge them for how they're living their life. It comes down to this simple statement: "What are you going to do about Jesus? God so loved the world that He gave his only begotten Son, that whoever believes on Him would not perish, but will have everlasting life. You can receive Him or you can reject Him. If you reject Him, this is the result. If you receive Him, this is the result. What are you going to do about Jesus?"

When you lead someone to Jesus, it will not only be the most important day in his or her life, but also one of the most fulfilling and joy-filled days of your life. The Bible says even the angels will rejoice. There will be a party in heaven because of your obedience to reach out and win your friends and family. You will please God. You will save a life, and God will bless your life as well.

— DAY 27 —

The J12 Project

"Go ye therefore, and teach all nations, baptizing them in the name of the Father, and of the Son, and of the Holy Ghost."
— Matthew 28:19

You've prayed. You've been a friend. You've told people about Jesus. You've introduced them to Him and helped them pray a salvation prayer. Now what? What happens after they receive Jesus? Do you just say, "Congratulations! Now find a good church home, and God bless you"? Or do you have a greater responsibility than that? When a mother spends nine months waiting for her baby to come and goes through twelve hours of labor, she doesn't leave the baby in the nursery. That new life needs care. You've given birth to a baby, too—a spiritual one—and God gives you a role in bringing that new life to maturity.

That is what the J12 Project is that we've launched through our church. It means, "Be like Jesus and get your twelve," or simply, "Make disciples." J12 is more than a motto, logo, creed, or song. J12 is a movement fueled by revelation of God's Word. Each of us needs to embrace that revelation because when we do, when it is burning on the inside of us, we will make disciples and win our city.

So, how do you start? You develop three disciples who will each develop three disciples, and then you will have reached twelve for Jesus.

We chose twelve for several reasons. First, twelve is the number of government in Scripture. Second, Jesus raised up twelve disciples.

However, the focus is not on the number twelve but on the making of disciples. If you get fifteen disciples, great! If you get your twelve tomorrow, you are not done. Making disciples—plural—is part of who you are, so don't stop at twelve. When you get to eternity and stand before the King of kings and He pulls out the book, He should be able to see that you made disciples.

Jesus said, "Ye have not chosen me, but I have chosen you, and ordained you, that ye should go and bring forth fruit, and that your fruit should remain" (John 15:16). In Matthew 28:19, He said, "Go and make disciples of all the nations" (NLT). Fruit. Disciples. Another word we might use is *results*. Jesus is talking about souls. He's talking about you winning someone to Jesus and then helping them stay in Jesus. The last thing you want is to run into that person six months down the

> ### If we as the body of Christ actively witness to people and make disciples who make disciples, that is how we will win the world. It can't happen any other way.

road and find them living as if they never received Him and instead went right back out into the world.

God doesn't want fruit that withers. He wants fruit that remains. He wants people who receive Him into their lives and continue to walk with Him for the rest of their lives. In fact, He wants them to go a step further. He wants them to start producing fruit for Him, too.

If we as the body of Christ actively witness to people and make disciples who make disciples, that is how we will win the world. It can't happen any other way. That's the way Jesus said it would happen. If, however, we don't have time or don't make it a priority, then the world around us is going to go to hell. And we will go before God in heaven one day, and He won't be very pleased with that aspect of our lives.

I want to give you three steps to help you make disciples.

Connect

You've just led someone to the Lord. They're excited; you're excited; now what? The first thing you have to do is connect that new person to others in the body of Christ. On the day of Pentecost, when 120 believers led three thousand people to Jesus, they didn't just say, "You all are the new guys, so you all meet over here. We original ones are going to meet over there. We'll see you every few months at the potluck." Acts 2:42 says they "continued stedfastly in the apostles' doctrine and fellowship, and in breaking of bread, and in prayers." Somebody took those new believers by the hand and said, "Come on over to my group. Peter's gonna preach. Come on, let's go hear him." Remember, this was only a few weeks after Jesus had risen. These 120 original believers knew what to do because Jesus taught them. They knew they had to take in these brand-new believers and make them a part of their lives—challenge them, mentor them, and live Jesus before them.

There's power in being a mentor. And if there's anyone who needs that type of attention, it's someone who just received Jesus as Lord of their life. If you can help them understand important lessons when they start off, they will hold on to them for the rest of their lives.

This was especially important in the world they were living in—and the world we are beginning to live in today—where believers were persecuted for what they believed. The 120 knew that the three thousand had made a decision that could land them in prison or even cost them their lives. The amount of pressure they were about to face could cause them to walk away from their new life unless they had strong, older believers around them.

Acts 2:46 tells us that the new believers were brought to the temple and to small groups. They did life together and brought the new people in to do life together with them. It's important for you to take people to church, but small groups are also important. When you take people to a small group setting, it's the perfect atmosphere for them to meet other believers and see that they are normal, see how they are living, and see what God has done for them. You've connected them.

Grow

The second thing you want to do is help them grow. Paul wrote, "My little children, of whom I travail in birth again until Christ be formed in you" (Gal. 4:19). He told Timothy, "The things that thou hast heard of me among many witnesses, the same commit thou to faithful men, who shall be able to teach others also" (2 Tim. 2:2).The word *commit* means "to deposit." Paul told Timothy to take the truths he learned and turn around and deposit them into the hearts of "faithful men." First Peter 2:2 says, "As newborn babes, desire the sincere milk of the word, that ye may grow thereby." You can help new believers grow by encouraging consistent church attendance, teaching God's Word in your small groups, and having personal conversations with them. Notice that you cannot deposit what you have not received, and when you do deposit it in someone else, it will cause them to grow. What do you want them to grow into? A disciple, so that they turn around, as Paul told Timothy, and teach others.

Send

"Then said Jesus to them again, Peace be unto you: as my Father hath sent me, even so send I you" (John 20:21). Every Christian should reach a point in their walk with God where they are going out to win their world just like you won them. It's up to us to encourage them to do so. This is how you win the world for Christ. You are a true disciple when you bear much fruit for Jesus, when you win souls, connect, disciple, and send them out to win their world. All you really have to do is save your world one person at a time. When you embrace that revelation, when it is burning inside you, you will make disciples and win your city and your world for Him.

I want to encourage you to follow God's strategy to save your world. Win someone in your world. Connect them. Grow them. Send them. Get your twelve one at a time, and together we will help God save the world.

GOD'S FUTURE FOR ME

1. What did you learn in this section that made you stop and re-evaluate your life as a believer?

   _____

   _____

   _____

   _____

2. Did the Holy Ghost convict you of anything on Day 23 or 24?

   _____

   _____

   _____

3. At the end of the last section, you updated your understanding of what God's future for you is. How will you revise it now that you've learned more about your role in saving the world?

   _____

   _____

   _____

   _____

4. Quote two Scriptures, one from the Old Testament and one from the New Testament, that shows that God wants you to help save the world around you.

   _____

   _____

   _____

   _____

5. Who have you led to the Lord that you need to follow up with? What specific ways can you disciple them?

   _____

_____

_____

_____

_____

6. List the verses that God has quickened to you during this section. Use them as declarations during the next week to remind yourself of God's promises to you about your future.

_____

_____

_____

_____

— DAY 28 —
Focus on the Future

[They] confessed that they were strangers and pilgrims
on the earth.

— Hebrews 11:13

There was a couple in Michigan who often talked about what they would do when the time came for one of them to die. They agreed that if the other one saw a look in their eyes that let them know they had seen the glory, they wouldn't try to resuscitate them but would just let them go. And that's exactly what happened. The husband was dying, and the wife was trying to resuscitate him. Suddenly she saw a look on his face and knew he had just seen the glory. So she stopped and let him step into eternity.

God has prepared for us a wonderful life throughout eternity. We are in seed time right now on the earth, but there is a harvest time coming. Thank God for seed time, but we will really get to rejoice in harvest time when we've stepped into eternity.

God's will is that you keep your eyes
fixed on eternity above all else. Focus
on the future—your ultimate future.

During the past twenty-eight days, you've learned about many lifestyle changes that God may be calling you to make in order to participate in His plans for your future. Eternity is the ultimate part of your future, and you must constantly focus on that. Many people in this world are focused on the now (believers as well as non-believers), but God's will is that you keep your eyes fixed on eternity above all else. Focus on the future—your ultimate future.

Hebrews 11 is often called the Faith Hall of Fame, where we read about those who went before us: Abraham, David, Moses, Joseph, Isaac, Sarah, and many others. They lived the lifestyle of the rich and righteous that we've studied. They may not have started off like that, but they eventually lived their lives in a way that pleased God. They all lived at different times, and they lived very different lives from each other, but there is one thing all of them did: "These all died in faith" (v. 13). If God highlighted these individuals as an example to us, that tells me we ought to die in faith, too. What does that mean? They died believing something. When they took their last breath, it was a breath of faith believing in something, "not having received the promises" (v. 13). This is a seemingly confusing verse because we know that many of them did receive what God promised them. Abraham received the promise of his son; David became king. In fact, verse 33 talks about these same individuals and says they obtained promises.

The writer is not talking about the specific promise God gave them for their specific situations. He is talking about a promise that was greater than that—the promises that were connected to the promise of the Messiah, Jesus, and what He would bring to them. Ultimately, that promise was a promise of salvation and an eternity in heaven. "Not having received the promises, but having seen them afar off… embraced them, and confessed that they were strangers and pilgrims on the earth" (v. 13). They walked around saying things like Jesus said. "I am not of this world," Jesus said of Himself (John 17:14). He said the same thing about His disciples: "They're not of this world, Father. That's why the world hates them" (see verse 14).

If you're not of this world, where are you of? These individuals believed they were of another world. They believed they were citizens of another kingdom. Meanwhile, here on the earth, they walked around as strangers, foreigners, aliens, and pilgrims.

It's the same with you. Your spirit was recreated when you made Jesus Christ the Lord of your life. It was not made on the assembly line of hell anymore. It was made on the assembly line of heaven. If you had a stamp on your heart and somebody could see it, it would say, "Made in New Jerusalem." You aren't of this place. You are from above. You are of heaven, and you're just passing through this place.

For they that say such things declare plainly that they seek a country. And truly, if they had been mindful of that country from whence they came out, they might have had opportunity to have returned. But now they desire a better country, that is, an heavenly: wherefore God is not ashamed to be called their God: for he hath prepared for them a city.

— Hebrews 11:14–16

The word *seek* in this passage means "to search out, to crave." The word *country* refers to a fatherland or a heavenly home. They were actively seeking out their real homeland. If they really didn't want to follow God anymore or pay the high price, God would have given them the opportunity to go right back where they came from—but they didn't want that, and God isn't ashamed of them.

Doesn't that make you wonder what we do that can make God ashamed of us? Clearly, it's when we get out of faith. These are people saying they are strangers and pilgrims, living their lives in a way to ensure that heaven would be their home—even though they had no natural evidence that there even is a heaven or an afterlife. They were living their lives based solely on what God told them.

New Jerusalem

Jesus said this about heaven: "In my Father's house are many mansions....I go to prepare a place for you" (John 14:2). The New Jerusalem has been the longest construction project in the history of the world. We can go back to Isaiah 54, when the New Jerusalem was barren and without children. There were no people in the New Jerusalem because Jesus had to die for them to come on in.

When a mother is pregnant, she may enjoy the time, but she's not hoping to stay pregnant forever. She's looking to that due date, and she's preparing herself for it. She prepares the house and the nursery, she has a baby shower, and she does many other things to prepare for the day that child will come.

We are individuals who follow the same example. We're living this life for God. We're producing for God. We're prospering in God, but we are looking forward to a day and a time when we enter eternity. How glorious it's going to be! The best thing you've ever experienced on this planet doesn't compare to what's waiting for you. And that's what you get to live in for all of eternity. If you want to know a glimpse of what heaven will be like, read Revelation 21. It is glorious!

Just remember that your job is to take as many people as you can with you. That's why you're still here. Work toward that day and keep your focus on the future. Whatever you are enduring here on the earth, remember: "For our light affliction, which is but for a moment, worketh for us a far more exceeding and eternal weight of glory; while we look not at the things which are seen, but at the things which are not seen: for the things which are seen are temporal; but the things which are not seen are eternal" (2 Cor. 4:17–19).

Look at what is eternal—at eternity. Keep your eye on that. Jesus said, "Watch therefore, for ye know neither the day nor the hour wherein the Son of man cometh" (Matt. 25:13). As you watch, keep these three keys in mind.

1. Maintain your salvation (see John 3:16). This life is just a vapor, a moment of time. What good is it if you gain the world but lose your soul? Fight the good fight of faith. Lay hold on eternal life (see 1 Timothy 6:12).

2. Increase your heavenly treasure. Jesus talked about laying up treasure in heaven and keeping your focus on that (see Matthew 6). He didn't say you shouldn't have any treasure on the earth but that your focus should be on your treasure in heaven. You lay up treasure in heaven by doing the good works the Bible teaches you ought to do, particularly giving.

3. Build the kingdom of God. Seek its expansion (see Colossians 4:11, AMP). You want to see the kingdom of God take more territory and therefore more souls. Build the kingdom. Witness to people yourself. Make disciples yourself, and also help others to do the same thing.

God says, "I know the plans I have for you... plans to prosper you and not to harm you, plans to give you hope and a future" (Jeremiah 29:11, NIV). With faith, there is a future. Keep your focus on the future—because God's future for you is spectacular!

ENDNOTES

1. For more on this, see Andy Stanley and Bill Willits, *Creating Community: Five Keys to Building a Small Group Culture* (Sisters, OR: Multnomah Publishers, 2004).

2. Craig Groeschel, *The Christian Atheist: Believing in God but Living as if He Doesn't Exist* (Grand Rapids, MI: Zondervan, 2010).

3. Rick Warren, *The Purpose-Driven Church: Growth Without Compromising Your Message and Mission* (Grand Rapids, MI: Zondervan, 1995).

RECOMMENDED RESOURCES

André Butler's other books and resources on how to live God's future for you:

Not in My House

Living Life to the Full

Winning the War Within

The Missing Element

Getting to Your Promised Land

God Is Making You Rich

Gaining Financial Freedom

Wealth of the Sinner, Harvest of the Just

The One Another Principle

Seedtime and Harvest: Receiving the Fullness of Your Harvest

God's Plan for the Church

God's Plan for the Single Saint

CONTACT INFORMATION

André Butler is dedicated to helping individuals experience the future God has for them. He accomplishes this mission through serving as senior pastor of Word of Faith International Christian Center in Southfield, Michigan, and through speaking engagements, "Your Future Now" broadcasts and podcasts, Facebook, Twitter, YouTube, CDs, MP3s, books, and much more. We invite you to visit www.GodsFutureforYou.com to connect with André Butler on Facebook, Twitter, and YouTube and to access videos, devotionals, and additional product offerings related to *God's Future For You*.

We also invite you to be a guest at Word of Faith:

Word of Faith

20000 W. Nine Mile Road

Southfield, MI 48075

www.wordoffaith.cc

IF YOU'RE A FAN OF THIS BOOK, PLEASE TELL OTHERS . . .

- Write about *God's Future for You* on your blog, Twitter, MySpace, and Facebook page.

- Suggest *God's Future for You* to friends.

- When you're in a bookstore, ask them if they carry the book. The book is available through all major distributors, so any bookstore that does not have *God's Future for You* in stock can easily order it.

- Write a positive review of *God's Future for You* on www.amazon.com.

- Send my publisher, HigherLife Publishing, suggestions on Web sites, conferences, and events you know of where this book could be offered at media@ahigherlife.com.

- Purchase additional copies to give away as gifts.

CONNECT WITH ME . . .

To learn more about *God's Future for You*, please contact me at:

Word of Faith

20000 W. Nine Mile Road

Southfield, MI 48075

www.wordoffaith.cc

You may also contact my publisher directly:

HigherLife Publishing

400 Fontana Circle

Building 1 – Suite 105

Oviedo, Florida 32765

Phone: (407) 563-4806

Email: media@ahigherlife.com